"In an increasingly global society, knowledge of other cultures and languages is crucial for optimal functioning. Many deaf and hard of hearing people face considerable challenges in this global society, an important one being their lack of proficiency in foreign languages such as English. This well written, pioneering work about teaching English as a foreign language to deaf and hard of hearing students is an important step to change this situation for the better."

Harry Knoors, *Professor of Deaf Education,*
Radboud University, The Netherlands

"*English as a Foreign Language for Deaf and Hard of Hearing Learners: Teaching Strategies and Interventions* selectively and effectively presents multiple perspectives, viewpoints and beliefs on teaching English to DHH students. The book is an impressive example of a long-awaited approach to teaching students with functional diversity: one that presents classroom-relevant research that will support teachers and professionals working with DHH students. The interventions and strategies presented in the volume reflect the contributors' life-time experience with DHH students making it a valuable resource for future practitioners. This book is a must for researchers interested in language teaching innovation."

Mari Carmen Campoy Cubillo, *PhD*
Jaume I University, Spain

English as a Foreign Language for Deaf and Hard of Hearing Learners

This book outlines best practices and effective strategies for teaching English as a foreign language to D/deaf and hard of hearing (DHH) students. Written by a group of researchers and experienced practitioners, the book presents a combination of theory, hands-on experience, and insight from DHH students.

The book brings together a variety of tried and tested teaching ideas primarily designed to be used for classroom work as a basis for standby lessons or to supplement courses. Placing considerable emphasis on practical strategies, it provides educators and practitioners with stimulating ideas that facilitate the emergence of fluency and communication skills. The chapters cover a wide range of interventions and strategies including early education teaching strategies, using sign bilingualism in the classroom, enhancing oral communication, speech visualization, improving pronunciation, using films and cartoons, lip-reading techniques, written support, and harnessing writing as a memory strategy.

Full of practical guidance grounded in theory, the book will be a useful resource for English teachers and all those involved in the education of deaf and hard of hearing learners across the world, including researchers, student teachers, newly qualified teachers, school supervisors, and counsellors.

Ewa Domagała-Zyśk is a researcher and lecturer at John Paul II Catholic University of Lublin (KUL), Poland and its Centre for Deaf and Hard of Hearing Education. She was a pioneer of teaching English as a foreign language to deaf university students in Poland.

Nuzha Moritz is Associate Professor of English language and phonetics at the University of Strasbourg, France. Her current research interest lies in English varieties and speech intelligibility by deaf and hard of hearing learners.

Anna Podlewska is an assistant professor in the Department of Foreign Languages at the Medical University of Lublin, Poland, where she has been teaching English and Polish for medical purposes to students of medicine and allied health sciences.

Routledge Research in Special Educational Needs

This series provides a forum for established and emerging scholars to discuss the latest debates, research and practice in the evolving field of Special Educational Needs.

Books in the series include:

English as a Foreign Language for Deaf and Hard of Hearing Learners
Teaching Strategies and Interventions
Edited by Ewa Domagala-Zysk, Nuzha Moritz, and Anna Podlewska

Understanding the Voices and Educational Experiences of Autistic Young People
From Research to Practice
Craig Goodall

Adult Interactive Style Intervention and Participatory Research Designs in Autism
Bridging the Gap between Academic Research and Practice
Lila Kossyvaki

The Global Convergence of Vocational and Special Education
Mass Schooling and Modern Educability
John G. Richardson, Jinting Wu, and Douglas M. Judge

Job Satisfaction of School-Based Speech-Language Pathologists
Insights to Inform Effective Educational Leadership
Kimberly A. Boynton

For more information about this series, please visit: www.routledge.com/Routledge-Research-in-Special-Educational-Needs/book-series/RRSEN

English as a Foreign Language for Deaf and Hard of Hearing Learners

Teaching Strategies and Interventions

Edited by Ewa Domagała-Zyśk, Nuzha Moritz, and Anna Podlewska

Routledge
Taylor & Francis Group

LONDON AND NEW YORK

First published 2021
by Routledge
2 Park Square, Milton Park, Abingdon, Oxon OX14 4RN

and by Routledge
605 Third Avenue, New York, NY 10158

Routledge is an imprint of the Taylor & Francis Group, an informa business

British Library Cataloguing-in-Publication Data
A catalogue record for this book is available from the British Library

Library of Congress Cataloging-in-Publication Data
A catalog record for this book has been requested

ISBN: 978-0-367-75354-2 (hbk)
ISBN: 978-0-367-75356-6 (pbk)
ISBN: 978-1-003-16217-9 (ebk)

Typeset in Times New Roman
by Apex CoVantage, LLC

Contents

List of figures   ix
List of contributors   x
Preface   xiii
EWA DOMAGAŁA-ZYŚK, NUZHA MORITZ, AND ANNA PODLEWSKA

**Introduction: State of the art of research on teaching
English as a foreign language to DHH learners**   1
EWA DOMAGAŁA-ZYŚK, NUZHA MORITZ, AND ANNA PODLEWSKA

**PART 1
Strategies and interventions for comprehensive input**   **15**

1   **To speak or not to speak? Speech and pronunciation
    of deaf and hard of hearing students learning English
    as a foreign language**   17
    EWA DOMAGAŁA-ZYŚK

2   **Phonic reading as a strategy in learning to read
    English as a foreign language for deaf and hard
    of hearing pupils**   32
    PATRICIA PRITCHARD

3   **Using cartoons as a strategy for enhancing oral
    communication in EFL classes for deaf and hard
    of hearing students**   45
    NUZHA MORITZ

4   **Bringing film to English as a foreign language for
     the deaf and hard of hearing class**   54
     ANNA PODLEWSKA

PART 2
Contexts and outcomes   79

5   **Individual differences in deaf learners' second
     language acquisition**   81
     JITKA SEDLÁČKOVÁ

6   **Deaf schoolchildren, adolescents, and adults on
     methods and strategies that work for them when
     learning foreign languages**   93
     EDIT H. KONTRA

7   **Adult deaf and hard of hearing people on learning
     English as a foreign language – international
     experiences and recommendations**   110
     PAULINA LEWANDOWSKA

     **Conclusion: Teaching English as a foreign language
     to DHH learners – future research and practical
     perspectives**   128
     EWA DOMAGAŁA-ZYŚK, NUZHA MORITZ, AND ANNA PODLEWSKA

     Index   132

Figures

4.1 Fingerspellings of ten vocabulary items from the *Word as Image* video   61
7.1 Type of school at each stage of education   115
7.2 Frequency of using English in everyday life   117

Contributors

Ewa Domagała-Zyśk is a university professor in the Department of Education at the John Paul II Catholic University of Lublin. After her studies, she worked as a pedagogue and an English teacher in a J.Ch. Andersen Therapeutic School for children with special educational needs. Since 1998, she has been working as a researcher and lecturer at KUL and its Centre for Deaf and Hard of Hearing Education. She was a pioneer of teaching English as a foreign language to deaf university students in Poland, starting her work with a specialist and innovative *English for the Deaf and Hard of Hearing* course in 1999. She is the author of more than 40 empirical papers on that issue and more than 50 presentations at international conferences and is an editor of *English as a foreign language for the deaf and hard of hearing persons in Europe* (2013, Lublin: Wydawnictwo KUL) and (together with E. Kontra) *English as a foreign language for deaf and hard-of-hearing persons. Challenges and strategies* (2016, Newcastle upon Tyne: Cambridge Scholars Publishing).

Edit H. Kontra, formerly affiliated with Eötvös Loránd University, Budapest, is currently an associate professor in the Department of English Language and Literature at János Selye University, Komarno, Slovakia where she teaches English, Applied Linguistics, and ELT Methodology. Her recent research has focused on individual differences, language learning in dyslexia, and the deaf language learner. She has been involved in researching the foreign language learning situation of deaf and hard of hearing Hungarians since 2006.

Paulina Lewandowska is a PhD student at the John Paul II Catholic University of Lublin. Her research interests focus on deaf and hard of hearing people and their social and educational inclusion. She is the co-author of *Zdalne uczenie się i nauczanie a specjalne potrzeby edukacyjne – z doświadczeń pandemii Covid-19* [Distance learning and teaching and special educational needs – from the experience of the Covid-19 pandemic] with the chapter *Dostępność edukacji zdalnej dla uczniów z niepełnosprawnością słuchową w klasach IV–VIII* [Accessibility of distance learning for students with hearing loss in classes IV–VIII]. She is also Secretary of the International Federation of Hard of Hearing Young People (IFHOHYP) and Vice-President of the Association of Hard of Hearing People and CI Users SUITA.

Nuzha Moritz is an associate professor of English language and phonetics in the Department of Applied Modern Languages at the University of Strasbourg. She has a PhD in Linguistics/specialized in Phonetics and an MA in English language and pedagogy. She has been teaching English as a foreign language since 1995 in different universities and institutes while preparing her PhD, and since 2001 as an associate professor at the University of Strasbourg. Her current research interest lies in English varieties and speech intelligibility by deaf and hard of hearing learners. She has participated in several international conferences, presenting her current work on deaf and hard of hearing speech intelligibility. She is also involved in pedagogical work at her university, seeking to develop aural activities for deaf and hard of hearing students.

Anna Podlewska, Ph.D., is an assistant professor in the Department of Foreign Languages at the Medical University of Lublin. She is also affiliated with the Institute of Pedagogy and the Centre for the Deaf and Hard of Hearing Education at the John Paul II Catholic University of Lublin. An experienced teacher, material writer, and teacher trainer, she has taught different age groups at all proficiency levels. Her experience involves teaching medical and business English. Her research interests focus on the use of cued speech to support language skills development in English language instruction for students who are deaf and hard of hearing.

Patricia Pritchard qualified as a teacher in England in 1972. After moving to Norway, she has worked in the classroom for over 20 years with the deaf and hard of hearing learners. She has worked on the development of methods for the teaching of English to deaf pupils, and the national curriculum for hearing-impaired pupils. Today, she is an educational advisor for teachers of the hearing impaired and is a textbook author. Her thesis for her master's degree was about the level of understanding of British Sign Language of Norwegian fourth grade deaf pupils. She has adapted assessment materials on communicative competence and developed materials for assessing the language environment for mainstreamed hearing-impaired children, as well as materials for assessing pupils' knowledge of English speech sounds and writing patterns. Patricia regularly lectures to teachers and parents on different areas of deaf education and sign bilingualism.

Jitka Sedláčková studied English language and literature at the Faculty of Arts, Masaryk University, Brno, Czech Republic. In the course of her studies, she became interested in English language teaching from both the practical and theoretical points of view. In 2008, she started teaching English to DHH students at the Masaryk University. She finished her PhD research focused on the reading of deaf learners in EFL in 2016. She works as a teacher trainer at the Department of English and American Studies and is a lecturer and methodologist at the Support Center for Students with Specific Needs at Masaryk University in Brno.

Preface

Ewa Domagała-Zyśk, Nuzha Moritz,
and Anna Podlewska

Almost every text on deaf and hard of hearing (DHH) students' education starts with enumerating and analyzing various medical, social, informational, and technological changes from recent years which have altered the educational opportunities for this group of students. While it is commonly agreed that digital hearing aids, cochlear implants, computer software, and internet databases have empowered DHH individuals to communicate and access knowledge in a variety of ways we may not have thought possible even as recently as 30 years ago, technology does have limitations, and classrooms in schools and universities might still be challenging environments for DHH learners. Similarly, even though educational approaches such as inclusion or diversity-sensitive education do affect the everyday functioning of DHH people, it is not easy to find their direct implementation in educational practice. Graduates of initial teacher training courses still tend to teach the way they were taught when at their schools, not the way they have been instructed to teach at university (Knoors & Marschark, 2014). Common stereotypes and labels of DHH students themselves and their cognitive capabilities are still prevailing, even in "updated" educational resources. What is more, it was noticed that paradoxically, contemporary educational DHH research rarely directly supports teachers and professionals, concentrating more on the "research for research's sake" model, deprioritizing the notion that every research should be *for* practice, not *beside* it:

> Researchers have often overlooked providing advice on valid and reliable instructional practices in favor of promoting one or another belief system. In addition, research has tended to be conducted in pursuit of an empirical question for which no follow-through was intended. Classroom relevant research is what we need.
>
> (Easterbrooks & Maiorana-Basas, 2015, p. 149)

The educational outcomes of DHH students are diverse and there is a common conviction that they should be better. Even if we agree that there was never in history a better time to be a DHH person (Marschark & Knoors, 2015), there is much to be done in order to make use in education of technological and social advancements to guarantee DHH students a high-quality education. It is not surprising that in this context, professionals increasingly argue for research designed expressly for DHH education. This can facilitate the development of evidence-based DHH education and enable trainees, newly trained teachers, and novice practitioners to devise specific teaching strategies and interventions based on documented prior educational successes. A comprehensive reference on this might then be widely implemented and evaluated, and, if need be, revised and improved (Knoors & Marschark, 2016). This model of research and education may be designed through close collaboration between researchers and teachers, with direct support from DHH students and their families. It is more and more commonly agreed and proclaimed that "the education of the DHH population will profit if we succeed in closing the gap between research and practice" (Knoors & Marschark, 2014).

The present book has been designed and written in this perspective by researchers who are either DHH teachers themselves or who cooperate closely with DHH educators. It was written for DHH teachers to offer them "classroom relevant research" (Easterbrooks & Maiorana-Basas, 2015) and support them in their effort to adjust their teaching practice to the diverse needs of today's DHH students. Studies show that teachers adopt new strategies and teaching methods more willingly when they are co-created by teachers and researchers and when they really meet the needs of students and teachers (Abbott, Walton, Tapia, & Greenwood, 1999). The evidence presented in this book was gathered during numerous classes with DHH students – and that made us courageous enough to share it with others.

As the title suggests, we concentrate on only one aspect of DHH education – teaching English as a foreign language (EFL). The strategies all come from countries where English is not a national or official language but is obligatorily taught as a contemporary *lingua franca* of science, education, and leisure. The opportunity of learning foreign languages seems to be taken for granted nowadays. In general, students understand the meaning of language education – especially of learning EFL – and enjoy being able to use foreign languages in education, work, and leisure time. The need to use English fluently is nowadays a very basic demand in education and the job market, not only in English-speaking countries, but also in a vast number of others. English is the language of global knowledge transmission, both in academia and in business – many international companies require it on an everyday basis. This creates a serious challenge for DHH students; in order to be successful in education and work, they have to master not only their national language but also English (Domagała-Zyśk, 2013; Archbold, 2015).

One may think that teaching EFL to DHH learners should not be too difficult a task – there are plenty of teaching resources in English-speaking countries for students of any age who learn English as their national language. However, it is not that simple. For most DHH students educated in continental Europe, their experience with EFL is significantly different from their L1 experience or the experience of learning a foreign language spoken in the surrounding community. This is hardly conducive to acquisition understood as the gradual development of ability in a language which occurs without conscious effort. To put it another way, for those who live in the USA, Canada, the UK, or Australia, for example, learning English as a national language means being "bathed" in this language. Even if they cannot hear it well, they spot it on every corner, and they live in a community that can help them in deciphering the meaning of English signs, texts, forms, web pages, or TV programs. If you learn EFL in a country where English is not used on an everyday basis   and you cannot hear it – usually you learn it only during your weekly class. You neither learn it "out of the corner of your ear" – because you cannot hear it well in spontaneous, incidental situations, nor "out of the corner of your eye" – because it is not evident in everyday situations in your local area.

One may also argue that reading (books, articles, and online texts) may make up for that. However, our years of experience of teaching DHH students have shown us that the English of books or websites – approached without human support – for our DHH students resembles not *bath* but *flood*, which everybody tries to avoid. To make matters worse, the fact remains, and has remained for several decades now, that apart from very few honorable exceptions, private language schools are not prepared to enroll DHH students in modern foreign language courses. A lack of fundamental knowledge about the functioning of this group of learners, as well as a dearth of appropriately adapted teaching materials contribute to this disadvantage in the language education market. Our students have to make the best of regular English classes at schools and universities – these classes are often the only opportunity they have to master English. For us it means a great challenge: to deliver teaching of the highest possible quality so as to maximize our students' chances not only to *pass* certain exams, but to *possess* language skills to the utmost.

Those who start their career as DHH English teachers may also feel at a loss and perceive their situation as being tossed into deep water without having basic swimming skills. The authors of this book also experienced this feeling several years ago starting their teaching careers in Hungary, France, Poland, Norway, and Czechia. Back in the 90s, it was even questioned whether DHH students could learn foreign languages, as it was believed that their problems were connected with lack of language. ("It is not the voice, – but the word which is the real problem of deaf students",

R.O. Cornett, a former president of Gallaudet University, once said). Since then, many things have changed – the methodology of teaching English as a foreign language has been described in many texts, among them two books published by our team: *English as a foreign language for deaf and hard of hearing persons in Europe* (ed. E. Domagała-Zyśk) and *English as a foreign language for deaf and hard of hearing persons – challenges and strategies* (ed. by E. Domagała-Zyśk and E. Kontra). Methodological work on principles and strategies for EFL teachers of DHH learners has also been undertaken by other researchers and teachers whose experiences we also find very meaningful, in Japan (Quay, 2005); Germany (Eitzen & Bartz, 2016); Finland (Kelly, Dufva, & Tapio, 2015); and Canada (Darroch 2013), France (Bedoin 2011), the USA (Liao 2010), Chile (Rodriguez, Munoz, Quezada, & Nopay, 2017).

The book *English as a foreign language for deaf and hard of hearing learners – teaching strategies and interventions* aims to be an updated source for all who are interested in improving the quality of language education for DHH people, including researchers, newly qualified teachers, school supervisors, counselors, and students. The international group of authors from Poland, Norway, Hungary, Czechia, and France do not only give an overview of the status quo of English classes for DHH learners in their homelands, but also share their best, most effective, and efficient strategies, techniques, methods, and materials with which they teach their students. It is hoped that these might be useful for English teachers of DHH learners across the world. This book aims to provide an incentive for both new and experienced teachers to re-examine how they work with their students, reflect on existing good practice, and develop practice further to reduce reliance on intuitive teaching. We want not only to teach English – we want it to be a part of DHH education, understood not only as knowledge and skills, but also as "a process of positive application of education in the life of an individual and a society" (Marschark & Knoors, 2015, p. 620). That is why we are so happy that our students exploit their English skills nowadays as active travelers, professionals working in international corporations, Erasmus exchange students in several countries (Nabiałek, 2013; Domagała-Zyśk, 2018; Sedláčková & Tothova, 2018), and participants of international associations and working groups advocating for DHH people's rights (e.g. the European Federation of Hard of Hearing People and the International Federation of Hard of Hearing Young People). This is possible because of our individual efforts as teachers, but we have also achieved something of a synergistic effect in our international collaboration. The importance of this type of cooperation is aptly summarized by Knoors and Marschark (2015b, p. 7):

[I]f we want our actions to result in meeting the challenges of deaf education in the 21st century and if we want to use resources to accomplish this goal efficiently, we simply cannot act only on our own – not as an individual special or mainstream school, not as an institute or university, not as a country. We have to collaborate internationally if we want DHH students to be successful as global citizens, competent in globally and locally important skills.

The present volume concentrates both on recent research and on teaching, in accordance with Knoors and Marschark (2015b, p. 5): "Designing and implementing sustainable interventions with respect to personal and financial resources is crucial". The texts are fully immersed in contemporary theory of EFL methodology, but at the same time, we have tried to be as practical as possible, which is why the chapters cover a wide range of interventions and strategies including early education teaching strategies; using sign bilingualism in the classroom; enhancing oral communication; improving pronunciation; using films, theme-based instruction, written support, and sign languages; and harnessing writing as a memory strategy. The book brings together a variety of tried and tested teaching ideas primarily designed to be used for classroom work as a basis for standby lessons or to supplement courses. Written by experienced teachers, the text provides novice educators and practitioners with stimulating ideas that facilitate the emergence of fluency and communication skills. The activities presented here encourage learners to take charge of interactions in a relaxed atmosphere and thus demonstrate the ease with which some of the key tenets of communicative language teaching can transfer into and energize DHH learners of EFL. All the previously mentioned strategies should be applied individually and on the basis of a good recognition of the pupils' needs – that is why the last chapter deals with the significance of individual differences among students.

As editors we would like to say a warm thank you to all the authors for their excellent contributions and cooperation during the process of preparing the book and their passion when they talk about their work and their students. We are overwhelmed by their devotion and we would like our readers to also experience this while studying each chapter of this book. Thanks are also due to our students, whose inquiring minds and commitment have motivated and inspired us to become better teachers.

References

Abbott, M., Walton, C., Tapia, Y., & Greenwood, C. R. (1999). Research to practice: A "blueprint" for closing the gap in local schools. *Exceptional Children, 65*(3), 339–352.

Archbold, S. (2015). Being a deaf student: Changes in characteristics and needs. In H. Knoors & M. Marschark (Eds.), *Educating deaf learners: Creating a global evidence base* (pp. 23–46). Oxford: Oxford University Press.

Bedoin, D. (2011). English teachers of deaf and hard of hearing students in French schools: Needs, barriers and strategies. *European Journal of Special Needs Education,* *26*(2), 159–175.

Darroch, K. (2013). Interpreting for deaf students in foreign language classes. *Association of Visual Language Interpreters of Canada News, 29*(2), 1–6.

Domagała-Zyśk, E. (2013). *Wielojęzyczni. Studenci niesłyszący i słabosłyszący w procesie uczenia się nauczania języków obcych.* Lublin: Wydawnictwo KUL

Easterbrooks, S. R., & Maiorana-Basas, M. (2015). Literacy and deaf and hard-of-hearing students. In H. Knoors & M. Marschark (Eds.), *Educating deaf learners: Creating a global evidence base* (pp. 149–172). Oxford: Oxford University Press.

Eitzen, B., & Bartz, M. (2016). Chancen und Grenzen des Einsatzes von American Sign Language (ASL) im Englischunterricht in der Sekundarstufe II – Erfahrungen und wissenschaftliche Erkenntnisse. *Horpad, 5,* 193–198.

Kelly, R., Dufva, H., & Tapio, E. (2015). Many languages, many modalities: Finnish Sign Language signers as learners of English. *AFinLAn Vuosikirja, 73,* 113–125.

Knoors, H., & Marschark, M. (2014). *Teaching Deaf Learners: Psychological and Developmental Foundations.* Oxford: Oxford University Press.

Knoors, H., & Marschark, M. (2015a). *Educating deaf learners: Creating a global evidence base.* Oxford: Oxford University Press.

Knoors, H., & Marschark, M. (2015b). Educating deaf students in a global context. In H. Knoors & M. Marschark (Eds.), *Educating deaf learners: Creating a global evidence base* (pp. 1–19). Oxford: Oxford University Press.

Knoors, H., & Marschark, M. (2016). *Evidence-based practices in deaf education.* Oxford: Oxford University Press.

Liao, Y. (2010). *Ugly ducklings or beautiful swans? Exploring the truths of hard of hearing students' foreign language learning experiences in the postsecondary education.* A dissertation sublimitted in partial fulfillment of the requirements for the degree of Doctoral of Philosophy. University of Wisconsin–Madison, UMI number: 3437303.

Marschark, M., & Knoors, H. (2015). Educating deaf learners in the 21st century. In H. Knoors & M. Marschark (Eds.), *Educating deaf learners: Creating a global evidence base* (pp. 617–648). Oxford: Oxford University Press.

Nabiałek, A. (2013). From a blackboard to an interactive whiteboard. Teaching English as a foreign language to deaf and hard of hearing students at Adam Mickiewicz University in Poznań. In: E. Domagała-Zyśk (Ed.), *English as a Foreign Language for Deaf and Hard of Hearing Persons in Europe,* Wydawnictwo KUL, Lublin.

Quay, S. (2005). Education reform and English teaching for the deaf in Japan. *Deafness and Education International, 7*(3), 139–153.

Rodriguez, N. A., Munoz, F. E., Quezada, E. I., & Nopay, I. S. (2017). *Applying pedagogical strategies for students with auditory disabilities in 8th grade A at Collegio Almirante Particio Lynch in Iquique.* Action Research project to obtain a degree of Profesor de Ingles para Ensenanza Pre-Escolar. Iquique, Chile: Universidad Arturo Prat.

Tóthová, L., & Sedláčková, J. (2018). Academic mobilities of students with hearing impairment: Welcoming the challenges with specialized online course of written English. Conference paper, 14th European Society for the Study of English Conference, Brno.

Introduction

State of the art of research on teaching English as a foreign language to DHH learners

Ewa Domagała-Zyśk, Nuzha Moritz, and Anna Podlewska

Foreign or second language acquisition (henceforth SLA) is a rather complex process, which is influenced by many factors. Several theories have been proposed in order to present a simplified view of this knotty process. In this introduction, we first group together some of the theories and methods that have played or still play an important role in SLA research. After that, a review of the current research on the art and methodology of teaching foreign languages to deaf and hard of hearing (DHH) people (called by some of us *surdo-glottodidactics*) is presented.

Behaviourism

In the field of SLA and learning in general, behaviourism or SSR (stimulus, response, and positive or negative reinforcement) was the dominant theory until 1965, with B.F. Skinner as its most well-known proponent. Behaviourists attach great importance to the environment of the learner. According to them, learning relies on *stimulus* coming from the environment, which causes a *response* that will then be consolidated thanks to the *reinforcement* provided by a reward. Thus, in a language learning situation, learners receive a stimulus in the form of listening to sounds or models proposed by the *entourage*, to which they respond by repeating or imitating the model, and receive a reward, for example, in the form of a response from their interlocutor. According to Lightbown and Spada (1993, p. 23), the final objective is to make the desired behaviour become a habit through repetition, until it is performed spontaneously:

> According to the behaviourists, all learning . . . takes place through the same underlying process, habit formation. Learners receive linguistic input from speakers in their environment, and positive reinforcement for their correct repetitions and imitations. As a result, habits are formed.

Most audio-oral methods with *structural exercises* are based on this theory. One positive aspect of behaviourist methods is the fact that the native language is not used during the process of teaching. However, in the methodology of teaching DHH persons, this might be questionable. Our experience led us to acknowledge the necessity of using the DHH person's national language or sign language, especially at first stages of learning a foreign language.

Language acquisition device

Beginning in the 1950s, linguist and philosopher Noam Chomsky rejected Skinner's theory and proposed a contradictory view of SLA. He brought language learning back to the forefront by defending the existence of an *innate* faculty or ability to acquire a language, which he called a *language acquisition device*. As summed up by Larsen-Freeman and Long (1999), Chomsky said that humans "possess a certain innate predisposition to induce the rules of the target language from the input to which they were exposed" (p. 57), and as infants they are "endowed with a highly sophisticated innate ability to learn languages" (p. 114).

One of the strengths of Chomsky's (1965) theory is its distinction between *competence* and *performance*. The innate possession of universal linguistic mechanisms is what he describes as the competence of the speaker, an intuitive and implicit knowledge of the language, while performance corresponds to speech. This distinction between competence and performance is one of the changes he brought to the field of language teaching. Although several linguists have questioned this distinction, Chomsky's theory has influenced many other theories with its concepts Chomsky, N. (2005). It also influences the methodology of teaching languages to DHH persons. Many linguists are convinced that DHH persons, though they may lack skill in language performance, at the same time might be fully competent users of any language.

Interlanguage

Larry Selinker adopted a new approach based on the learner's language transfer called *interlanguage*. He considers that the interlanguage is a unique intermediate system that is not a projection of the target language or the source language, but has its own unique characteristics that result from five cognitive processes:

- Language transfer: a speaker can transfer certain elements, rules, or subsystems of their first language to the second one.
- Transfer of training: the speaker can also transfer elements related to learning the target language.

- Strategies of SLA: certain elements in the interlanguage may be the consequence of strategies for learning the target language.
- Strategies of second language communication: other elements of an interlanguage result from communication strategies that learners adopt when speaking with native speakers of their target language.
- Overgeneralization of target language linguistics: an interlanguage can contain elements introduced through the learner that overgeneralize certain rules and semantic aspects of the target language.

(Selinker, 1972)

According to Selinker, SLA is fundamentally different from first language acquisition because of the propensity for *fossilization*, where the second language freezes in its development. The learner does not always reach the final stage of mastery of the target language, despite his continuous exposure to it, due to "fossilizable linguistic phenomena" that Selinker (1972, p. 205) defines as

linguistic items, rules, and subsystems which speakers of a particular native language will tend to keep in their interlanguage relative to a particular target language, no matter what the age of the learner or the amount of explanation and instruction he receives in the target language.

Interlanguages have many features in common with natural languages but present, in addition, specific characteristics which mainly arise from their instability and evolution. Selinker argues that fossilization is due primarily to the transfer of elements from the mother tongue. Other processes, such as communication strategies, can also cause fossilization: a learner may feel that their mastery of a target language is sufficient to be able to communicate in that language and thus may no longer care about forms deviating from the native norm.

Information processing

Cognitivists like R.C. Anderson (1983) consider SLA to be a complex cognitive process that requires the gathering of many small language units to build a whole. He developed what he calls the adaptive control of thought (ACT), where human intelligence is based on two representations of knowledge: *declarative*, which is stored in long term memory, and *procedural*, which corresponds to a progressive and continuous way of acquiring a language. Ellis (1994, p. 389) calls the ACT model

enormously complex . . . it is not possible to do justice to this complexity here. The central point to grasp is the theoretical claim that learning

begins with declarative knowledge which slowly become procedural-
ized, and that the mechanism by which this takes place is practice.

The ACT model has been very influential in cognitive approaches to SLA
Ellis, R. (1996).

Stephen Krashen's theory of SLA

In the methodology of teaching English to DHH learners, the most significant input comes from Stephen Krashen (1987, 1988, and others). According to his SLA theory, while learning language we do not need tedious drills
or extensive teaching about grammar rules. SLA requires *meaningful interaction in a target language* in which interlocutors are concerned not with
the grammar of the sentences, but with the meaning they are conveying.
This approach then guides the choice of methods and teaching strategies
which should supply *comprehensive input* in an environment low in anxiety
and fear. Krashen contrasts *language acquisition* with *language learning.*
While the former is based on each person's natural curiosity and motivation to gain knowledge, the latter describes the deductive, teacher-centered
situation of learning *about* the language. When a language has been *learnt*,
it allows one to pass an exam, but not necessarily to use the language in
everyday life. When a language has been *acquired*, it becomes a tool for
daily communication, education, employment, and entertainment.

It is not easy for a DHH learner to *acquire* a spoken language. They usually do not experience immersion even in their national language but have
to consciously learn *about* the language they are going to use. Nevertheless,
years of experience confirms that their psychological processes of language
acquisition are similar to those of the hearing population (cf. Domagała-
Zyśk, 2013a). As surdo-glottodidactics professionals, we agree that DHH
students are able to not only *learn about language*, but are able to *acquire
language*. In line with Krashen, second language teaching for DHH students should meet the following criteria:

*   Input must be natural, interesting, and meaningful for the students, but
    also compelling (Krashen, 2011) in terms of being one step beyond
    their current stage of language competence. This entails not only
    knowing the DHH students' passions and desires, but also the diver-
    sity of their language experiences (cf. *the personalization strategy*,
    Domagała-Zyśk, 2016b). The *compelling language* input (Krashen,
    2011) should be interesting enough that the student does not treat it
    merely as learning material for a language class, but as interesting con-
    tent in its own right. Learners are not consciously aware that their time

is being spent on learning a language, and nothing but the activity itself matters, which can be considered as experiencing "flow" (Csikszentmihalyi, 1990).

- Language acquisition strategies should acknowledge the influence of the affective filter. Krashen observed that a number of variables (like motivation, confidence, good self-image, low level of anxiety, and extroversion) may play a facilitative role in SLA. On the other hand, some features can raise the affective filter and form a "mental block" that prevents comprehensible input from being used. Emotion and affect should be included in the acquisition process as they raise motivation and enjoyment (cf. *emotionalisation strategy*, Domagała-Zyśk, 2016b).

- Krashen stressed the significance of both listening to and reading input, especially in conjunction with the stage guided self-selected reading technique (Krashen, 1994; Mason & Krashen, 2017; Cho, 2017). While listening to English is problematic for many DHH students, providing them with large amounts of optimal well-written input is crucial for their progress. When using cochlear implants (CIs) and hearing aids, many DHH students can participate in listening activities, so these should be included in their SLA process. If a DHH person can listen to her national language, there is usually no reason she cannot listen to a foreign language, especially in an acoustically comfortable environment (cf. Domagała-Zyśk, Chapter 1 of this volume).

- Some SLA tasks (especially formal assessment or exams) might be perceived by learners as mundane. An important factor of success in SLA is pleasure; as explained in Krashen's *pleasure hypothesis*: "those activities that are good for language acquisition are usually perceived by acquirers as pleasant" (Krashen, 1994, p. 299; cf. also Lao and Krashen, 2008). In order to be effective, teachers should provide enjoyable and meaning-focused activities. This rule also applies to DHH subjects, who usually have experienced many mundane tasks during their education. They deserve pleasure in the SLA process and their language successes should be celebrated and enjoyed as a most welcome reward.

- Traditional error correction is described by Krashen as ineffective, because making mistakes is perceived as a natural part of learning. It is better for error correction to happen incidentally (e.g. as self-correction). The most profitable part of language acquisition is practicing language and using it in meaningful utterances.

Teaching EFL to DHH students has strong roots in these classical theories and methodologies for teaching foreign languages. On the other hand,

6 Ewa Domagała-Zyśk, Nuzha Moritz and Anna Podlewska

surdo-glottodidactics has its own specific characteristics which are described in the following section.

The emergence of surdo-glottodidactics

Surdo-glottodidactics is a relatively young subdiscipline of glottodidactics.[1] Its origins can be traced back to applied linguistics and deaf studies. Etymologically, it derives from Latin *surdus*, meaning 'deaf', Greek *glotta* 'language', and *didaskein* 'to teach'. As a discipline, it is primarily concerned with the teaching of foreign languages to, and the learning of foreign languages by, DHH students. Its scope of interest also includes teacher training and the design and adaptation of teaching materials for use in foreign language instruction for DHH learners.

The term was introduced in the paper "Czy istnieje już surdoglottodydaktyka?" [Is there such a discipline as surdo-glottodidactics?] by Ewa Domagała-Zyśk in 2003. The beginnings of surdo-glottodidactics in Poland can be therefore associated with the John Paul II Catholic University of Lublin where the author of the aforementioned paper and one of the coeditors of this volume started conducting English as a foreign language (EFL) classes for DHH students in 1999. It was then that the need for establishing surdo-glottodidactics as a scientific discipline in its own right started to be voiced for the first time by educators in Poland and other European countries. Prior to that date, there was a dearth of information on the subject of foreign language instruction for DHH students. In fact, there was a tendency to think that this group of students should be exempted from foreign language classes (cf. Domagała-Zyśk, 2003; Mole, McColl, & Vale, 2005; Kontra, 2013; Podlewska, 2014). The lack of any systematic research aimed at developing a theoretical perspective on teaching foreign languages to DHH individuals led to a situation where their teachers had to work it out on their own. Consequently, teaching foreign languages to DHH individuals constitutes one of those spheres of education where practice is well ahead of theory.

Nevertheless, it is worthwhile to emphasize here that the practical experiences of European foreign language teachers working with DHH learners have been used in research for over two decades. The first European publications on this topic started appearing in the early 2000s and included the paper on surdo-glottodidactics and its research areas (Domagała-Zyśk, 2003); a practical guide for teaching and supporting deaf students in foreign language classes (Mole et al., 2005); and the proceedings of three international seminars (Janáková, 2005a, 2005b; Kellett Bidoli & Ochse, 2008). From the moment DHH individuals gained access to foreign language study, the researchers, many of whom were at the same time devoted practitioners, were very much aware that without an appropriate research base, there could not be effective practice. This awareness has led to the formation of an international research group that aims to conduct research in the field of surdo-glottodidactics, with a particular bend towards its implementation in Europe (see www.kul.pl/english-for-deaf-and-hard-of-hearing,art_74431.html). The group members are pioneers who understand the need for international collaboration between educational researchers and foreign language teachers working with DHH students. They have no pretense of offering a comprehensive account of how foreign languages should be taught to DHH individuals. Instead, they work together to bridge the gap between research and practice to produce more positive outcomes for DHH learners. (For a detailed discussion on the chasm between research and practice in special education, see Cawthon & Garberoglio, 2017; Cook & Odom, 2013; and Swanwick & Marschark, 2010).

Teaching foreign languages to the DHH population – a review of the research to date

The key underlying principle for maximizing learning outcomes for all students, not just DHH students, is for teachers to know about their learners' past educational experiences, learning styles, learning preferences, and ability. This knowledge makes it possible for teachers to use a broad repertoire of effective instructional and assessment strategies that can be differentiated according to how students learn and demonstrate their learning. In an effort to devise strategies that capitalize on learners' strengths, the practitioner research group described in the previous section has carried out a number of studies on DHH students' perspectives on foreign language learning. This research is based on the premise that learning foreign languages and being DHH can be part of the same positive experience. Moreover, as contributors to this volume attest, knowledge of a foreign language can have a beneficial impact on the psychosocial functioning of DHH students.

A particularly informative account of the foreign language learning experiences of Hungarian deaf students was given by Kontra (2013). This was a qualitative study using data from semi-structured interviews with members of the Deaf Community in Budapest. The respondents revealed their manifold struggle for equity in foreign language education.[2] The participants therefore advocated for the implementation of barrier-free education, where their national sign language is used across the curriculum, including in foreign language classes. This highlights the need for deaf teachers and other educators who can sign.

Research into the needs, strategies, and challenges of EFL teachers working with DHH students was conducted in France by Bedoin (2011).

The strategies she found include mixing the target and national language in teaching instruction, bolstering the students' aspirations and motivation, and providing both written and spoken input. She discovered that few teachers were adequately prepared for working with DHH students and strongly advocates for specialized teacher training.

The notion of equity in foreign language instruction for DHH learners was also discussed by Pritchard (2013) who conducted research in Norway where the curriculum allows these students a choice of the language they want to learn. They can choose between British Sign Language (BSL), American Sign Language (ASL), spoken English, or written English. Pritchard looked into deaf learners' acquisition of BSL. The results indicated that if learners were given adequate BSL input, they managed to grasp and understand the language even though their teachers were not language models.

There have been a number of studies that set out to explore the ways in which DHH learners can develop reading skills in foreign languages. Sedláčková and Fonioková (2013) examined cognitive and meta-cognitive strategies for acquiring L1 and L2 reading skills, and their possible application in foreign language instruction for DHH students. Sedláčková (2016) also presented an example of a framework for teaching reading strategies, developed for a series of interventions with deaf university students who were learning English. Using a qualitative approach and multiple case studies, the researcher posited that the conscious teaching of reading strategies leads to beneficial outcomes for deaf foreign language learners.

Moritz (2016) addressed the issue of oral communication and the speech intelligibility of DHH learners using a case study of two students by looking at their segmental and supra-segmental articulatory errors. Overall, the analysis confirmed that on the segmental level, consonant errors like substitution, omission, and devoicing are more harmful to intelligibility than vowel errors. This has implications for foreign language instruction and shows that teachers working with DHH foreign language learners need to have an adequate understanding of the nature of their learners' challenges.

In a series of studies conducted in various kinds of educational settings (primary and lower secondary school, and university), Domagała-Zyśk (2013b) found that DHH learners demonstrated only a limited ability to use English for practical communication. It is worthy of note, nonetheless, that this ability develops over time. The majority of DHH students who receive adequate intervention manage to increase their writing skills and use English in its written form to more effectively navigate the world they live in. Strategies for intervention include experiential learning, flipped instruction (Domagała-Zyśk, 2016a), vocabulary personalization and emotionalization, and semantic and morphological analysis of words (2016b).

The majority of the students participating in action research conducted by Domagała-Zyśk in 2001–2011 (Domagała-Zyśk, 2013, 2016a, 2016b) declared that it was their intention to speak English, which they did as far as they were able. Domagała-Zyśk advocates for further research, including international, longitudinal, and comparative works, into innovative teaching strategies that allow DHH students to acquire and produce the language they need for everyday use, education, and employment.

Podlewska (2014) conducted a large-scale investigation into the importance attached to mastering the four language elements (spelling, pronunciation, vocabulary, and grammar) as well as the four language skills (listening, reading, speaking, and writing) by DHH learners from different countries. An eight-item self-report was designed to measure the importance attached to various aspects of their foreign language proficiency. It was translated into a number of spoken as well as signed languages and distributed to DHH individuals as either written text or a video recording. The 123 respondents were all undergraduate or postgraduate students, and spanned a range of ages, nationalities, and degrees of hearing loss. The study demonstrated that DHH foreign language learners who had developed speech skills in their national languages wanted to speak in their target foreign languages as well. These results held across the groups regardless of first language background and suggest that DHH foreign language learners, if properly guided, want to and are capable of developing all language skills, including speaking.

Another study conducted by Podlewska (2016) focused on the potential benefits of using cued speech in EFL instruction for DHH university students (also see Bement & Quenin, 1998; Clark & Sacken, 1998; Podlewska, 2011, 2012, 2013; and Krakowiak, Domagała-Zyśk, & Podlewska, 2012). The four-year study was aimed at examining the effect of cued-speech-enhanced EFL instruction on the speech intelligibility scores of two highly motivated Polish university students. Twelve speech samples, which included oral reading, spontaneous speech, and language elicited by the researcher, were provided by the two DHH participants and later assessed by native and non-native listeners. Three samples from each set were captured on audio and video recordings after two years of cued-speech-enhanced EFL training and three more were captured after four years. The study indicated that in terms of content comprehension, pronunciation accuracy, and the percentages of target words correctly transcribed, both students received significantly better ratings for the recordings captured after four years of the enhanced training than for those captured after two years. These results suggest that the integration of pronunciation practice in EFL courses and the systematic use of cued speech may contribute to increased speech intelligibility for DHH students.

More recently, an action research case study conducted by Domagała-Zyśk and Podlewska (2019) focused on the oral communication strategies of DHH English learners. The results indicated that when they communicate orally in the target foreign language, DHH students use the same verbal, nonverbal, linguistic, and nonlinguistic stimuli as their hearing peers, alongside certain characteristic communication strategies. The researchers concluded that in order for the research outcomes to reach DHH learners in meaningful ways, foreign language teachers should integrate strategy awareness and practice into their pedagogy.

Whilst there have been two decades of research on teaching modern foreign languages to DHH students, surdo-glottodidactics is still at a nascent stage. The need is for researchers to clearly define the objectives, methodology, and terminology of the discipline in order to better respond to challenges such as limited generalizability due to small sample sizes and heterogeneous study populations. Teachers, in their turn, should be aware of the fact that no instructional practice is guaranteed to work for every student, so practitioners in the field need to validate the effectiveness of the interventions for each individual student.

Notes

1 The term *glottodidactics* was coined by Polish linguist Ludwik Zabrocki in the 1960s. It is mainly used in Polish and Greek educational contexts, whereas the Anglophone world prefers the term *foreign language teaching methodology*.
2 Equality and equity are two notions that are closely intertwined with the concept of fairness. Equality generally requires one to provide students with the same (equal) formats of information and ways to demonstrate learning (e.g. everyone watches the same subtitled video material, and everyone writes an essay for the assignment). Equity refers to offering varying formats of information, levels of support, and options for students to show what they have learnt (e.g. students can choose to explore information from a list of articles and videos; decide what, if any, form of accommodation is needed; access some digital study tools; and then choose to produce either a PowerPoint presentation, a short video, or an essay).

References

Anderson, R. C. (1983). *The architecture of cognition*. Cambridge, Mass. Harvard University Press.

Bedoin, D. (2011). English teachers of deaf and hard-of-hearing students in French schools: Needs, barriers and strategies. *European Journal of Special Needs Education*, *26*(2), 159–175. https://doi.org/10.1080/08856257.2011.563605

Bement, L., & Quenin, C. (1998). Cued speech as a practical approach to teaching Spanish to deaf and hard-of-hearing foreign language students. *Cued Speech Journal*, *6*, 40–56.

Cawthon, S. W., & Garberoglio, C. L. (Eds.). (2017). *Research in deaf education: Contexts, challenges, and considerations*. New York: Oxford University Press.

Cho, K. S. (2017). A student in Korea discovers the power of reading. *The International Journal of Foreign Language Teaching*, *12*(2), 9–14.

Chomsky, N. (1965). *Aspects of the theory of syntax*. Cambridge, MA: MIT Press.

Chomsky, N. (2005). *Nouveaux horizons dans l'étude du langage et de l'esprit*. Paris: Stock.

Chomsky, N., & Katz, J. (1975). On innateness: A reply to Cooper. *The Philosophical Review*, *84*(1), 70–71.

Clark, C., & Sacken, J. P. (1998). French cued speech: Teaching French in a mainstream college classroom. *Cued Speech Journal*, *6*, 57–70.

Cook, B. G., & Odom, S. L. (2013). Evidence-based practices and implementation science in special education. *Exceptional Children*, *79*(2), 135–144.

Crystal, D. (1997). *The Cambridge encyclopaedia of language*. Cambridge: Cambridge University Press.

Csikszentmihalyi, M. (1990). *Flow: The psychology of optimal experience*. New York: Harper Perennial.

Devaele, J. M. (2003). Compte rendu – hommage: l'œuvre de L. Selinker. *Linx*, *49*, 153–159.

Domagała-Zyśk, E. (2003). Czy istnieje już surdoglottodydaktyka? [Is there such a discipline as surdo-glottodidactics?]. *Języki obce w szkole*, *4*, 3–6.

Domagała-Zyśk, E. (2013a). *Wielojęzyczni. Studenci niesłyszący i słabosłyszący w procesie uczenia się nauczania języków obcych* (ss.420). Lublin: Wydawnictwo KUL.

Domagała-Zyśk, E. (2013b). Written English of Polish deaf and hard-of-hearing grammar school students. In E. Domagała-Zyśk (Ed.), *English as a foreign language for DHH persons in Europe* (pp. 163–179). Lublin: Wydawnictwo KUL.

Domagała-Zyśk, E. (2016a). Teaching English as a second language to deaf and hard-of-hearing students. In M. Marschark & P. E. Spencer (Eds.), *The Oxford handbook of deaf studies in language* (pp. 231–246). New York: Oxford University Press.

Domagała-Zyśk, E. (2016b). Vocabulary teaching strategies in EFL classes for deaf and hard of hearing students. In E. Domagała-Zyśk & E. H. Kontra (Eds.), *English as a foreign language for deaf and hard-of-hearing persons: Challenges and strategies* (pp. 135–152). Newcastle upon Tyne: Cambridge Scholars Publishing.

Domagała-Zyśk, E., & Podlewska, A. (2019). Strategies of oral communication of deaf and hard-of-hearing (DHH) non-native English users. *European Journal of Special Needs Education*. https://doi.org/10.1080/08856257.2019.158139

Ellis, R. (1986). *Understanding second language acquisition*. Oxford: Oxford University Press.

Ellis, R. (1994). *The Study of Second Language Acquisition*. Oxford University Press.

Gass, S., & Selinker, L. (1994). *Second language acquisition: An introductory course*. Hillsdale, NJ: Lawrence Erlbaum.

Janáková, D. (Ed.). (2005a). *Proceedings 2000. Teaching English to deaf and hard-of-hearing students at secondary and tertiary levels of education in the Czech Republic*. Prague: Eurolex Bohemia.

Janáková, D. (Ed.). (2005b). *Proceedings 2000. Teaching English to deaf and hard-of-hearing students at secondary and tertiary levels of education in the Czech Republic*. Prague: Eurolex Bohemia.

Kellett Bidoli, C. J., & Ochse, E. (Eds.). (2008). *English in international deaf communication*. Bern: Peter Lang.

Kontra, E. H. (2013). Language learning against the odds: Retrospective accounts by deaf adults. In E. Domagała-Zyśk (Ed.), *English as a foreign language for DHH persons in Europe* (pp. 93–112). Lublin: Wydawnictwo KUL.

Krakowiak, K., Domagała-Zyśk, E., & Podlewska, A. (2012). Cued speech – A tool to enhance development, education and full family life. In E. Domagała-Zyśk, D. Bis, & A. Rynio (Eds.), *Social and educational support in life-long human development* (pp. 141–160). Lublin: Wydawnictwo KUL.

Krashen, S. D. (1985). *The input hypothesis: Issues and implications*. New York: Longman.

Krashen, S. D. (1987). *Principles and practice in second language acquisition*. Prentice-Hall International.

Krashen, S. D. (1988). *Second language acquisition and second language learning*. Prentice-Hall International.

Krashen, S. D. (1994). The pleasure hypothesis. In J. Alatis (Ed.), *Georgetown University round table on languages and linguistics* (pp. 299–322). Washington, DC: Georgetown University Press.

Krashen, S. D. (2011). The compelling (not just interesting) input hypothesis. *The English Connection (KOTESOL)*, *15*(3), 1.

Lao, C., & Krashen, S. (2008). Do students like what is good for them? An investigation of the pleasure hypothesis with middle school students of Mandarin. *International Journal of Foreign Language Teaching*, *4*(2), 19–20.

Larsen-Freeman, D., & Long, M. H. (1999). *An Introduction to second language acquisition research*. London: Longman.

Lightbown, P., & Spada, N. (2006). *How Languages are Learned*. (3rd edition). Oxford: Oxford University Press.

Mason, B., & Krashen, S. (2017). Self-selected reading and TOEIC performance: Evidence from case histories. *Shitennoji Kiyo*, *63*, 469–475.

Mole, J., McColl, H., & Vale, M. (2005). *Deaf and multilingual*. Derbyshire, UK: Direct Learn Services.

Moritz, N. (2016). Oral communication and intelligibility of oral speech. In E. Domagała-Zyśk & E. H. Kontra (Eds.), *English as a foreign language for deaf and hard-of-hearing persons challenges and strategies* (pp. 9–22). Newcastle upon Tyne: Cambridge Scholars Publishing.

Podlewska, A. (2011). Educational technology and other learning resources in English language instruction for students with hearing impairment. In *Proceedings of the conference universal learning design, Brno 2011* (pp. 101–107). Brno: Masaryk University.

Podlewska, A. (2012). Adapatacja materiałów dydaktycznych w nauce języka angielskiego studentów z dysfunkcją słuchu [Adaptation of teaching materials in English language instruction for students with hearing impairments]. In Z. Palak,

D. Chimicz, & A. Pawlak (Eds.), *Wielość obszarów we współczesnej pedagogice specjalnej* (pp. 383–390). Lublin: Wydawnictwo UMCS.

Podlewska, A. (2013). The use of cued speech within an empirically-based approach to teaching English as a foreign language to hard-of-hearing students. In E. Domagała-Zyśk (Ed.), *English as a foreign language for deaf and hard of hearing persons in Europe* (pp. 181–196). Lublin: Wydawnictwo KUL.

Podlewska, A. (2014). Deaf and hard of hearing students' perspectives on foreign language proficiency. In E. Domagała-Zyśk (Ed.), *"Nie głos, ale słowo . . ." 4 developing language competence of people with hearing and speech disorders* (pp. 153–162). Lublin: Wydawnictwo KUL.

Podlewska, A. (2016). The use of cued speech to support the development of verbal language skills in English language instruction for deaf and hard-of-hearing students. In E. Domagała-Zyśk & E. H. Kontra (Eds.), *English as a foreign language for deaf and hard-of-hearing persons: Challenges and strategies* (pp. 23–40). Newcastle upon Tyne: Cambridge Scholars Publishing.

Pritchard, P. (2013). Teaching of English to deaf and severely hard-of-hearing pupils in Norway. In E. Domagała-Zyśk (Ed.), *English as a foreign language for DHH persons in Europe* (pp. 113–134). Lublin: Wydawnictwo KUL.

Sedláčková, J. (2016). Challenges of the reading comprehension development of deaf learners in the foreign language classroom: Putting theory into practice. In E. Domagała-Zyśk & E. H. Kontra (Eds.), *English as a foreign language for deaf and hard-of-hearing persons: Challenges and strategies* (pp. 109–134). Newcastle upon Tyne: Cambridge Scholars Publishing.

Sedláčková, J., & Fonioková, Z. (2013). Reading strategy instruction for deaf learners of English: Definitions, contexts and implications. In E. Domagała-Zyśk (Ed.), *English as a foreign language for DHH persons in Europe* (pp. 135–152). Lublin: Wydawnictwo KUL.

Selinker, L. (1972). Interlanguage. *International Review of Applied Linguistics, 10*, 219–231. https://doi.org/10.1515/iral.1972.10.1-4.209

Swanwick, R., & Marschark, M. (2010). Enhancing education for deaf children: Research into practice and back again. *Deafness and Education International, 12*(4), 217–235.

Part 1

Strategies and interventions for comprehensive input

1 To speak or not to speak? Speech and pronunciation of deaf and hard of hearing students learning English as a foreign language

Ewa Domagała-Zyśk

Introduction

Starting my teaching career as an English teacher of deaf and hard of hearing students, I was full of both excitement and fear. One of these fears was connected with teaching pronunciation and speaking to learners who were only partially able to speak their national spoken language. Then, I sought advice from Professor Boguslaw Marek, my teacher of English phonology and phonetics at the John Paul II Catholic University of Lublin. After listening patiently to my objections, he asked just two questions. The first was: "Do they speak Polish?" I answered affirmatively but pointed out that their pronunciation and speech intelligibility are sometimes far from ideal. His second question was: "Why should we forbid them to speak English?" That, I think, was the most important question in my teaching career. It is awfully true; I do not have any right to prevent anybody from using any language they want. The crucial issue is whether they want to.

The readers of this book surely know that DHH persons choose to communicate in a variety of modes. Some use manual communication as their only or main means of interacting with other people. Due to their type of hearing loss and educational background, they may not want to speak the majority spoken language. However, most DHH people nowadays are able to hear their native spoken language to some extent. They typically learn to speak and willingly use this method of communication in myriad educational and social contexts. Very often they do not know or use sign language. Such individuals tend to be interested in learning not only to read and write, but also to listen and speak in a foreign language.

This chapter discusses the speech and pronunciation challenges of DHH students and activities during EFL classes. The first part is devoted to pinpointing these barriers and challenges, and the second part describes some teaching methods and activities that promote DHH students' speaking skills and good pronunciation habits. Examples of my students' work and opinions are provided throughout the chapter. Though they are secondary school and university students, the strategies can also be adapted for younger learners.

Why it is it difficult for DHH people to learn English pronunciation?

Though the main impact of deafness from birth is the difficulty in learning and using spoken language, which is the type of language most commonly used by society in general (Marschark & Spencer, 2006; Archbold, 2015), spoken language development of deaf children may be more possible today than ever before (Marschark & Spencer, 2006). This has happened thanks to early diagnosis and intervention, the rapid development of technology (cochlear implantation at a very early age, good quality hearing aids, etc.), and DHH children being offered personalized care and education that gives them a higher chance of reaching their full cognitive potential.

Nowadays, spoken language development (especially in non-English speaking countries) entails not only national but also foreign language learning, and the younger generation in many countries is functionally bilingual, using English as a tool to access information, career opportunities, and entertainment.

The first successful attempts to teach foreign languages to DHH students were made naturally in the context of bilingual families, migration, and/or education in a bilingual or multilingual country: DHH children and young people in such contexts are exposed to and may acquire two or more spoken languages. The first formal foreign language classes for DHH learners started at Gallaudet University at the end of 19th century (Sutherland, 2008). This university has been providing foreign language education for many years within the Department of Foreign Languages, Literature, and Cultures, where Spanish, French, German, Italian, and Latin are taught, mainly in their written forms.

In most European countries, foreign language instruction has been obligatory for hearing students for several decades. However, up until the 1990s, DHH students were deprived of this possibility. It was not until then that foreign language classes for DHH students became available in non-English-speaking European countries (Domagała-Zyśk, 2003a). This teaching specialism is growing alongside research (cf. Domagała-Zyśk, 2003b; Janakova, 2005; Bajko, 2008; Kontra, 2013; Domagała-Zyśk, 2013a), thus paving the way for improved, evidence-based practice that addresses the linguistic challenges for DHH children and adults.

Speaking in a foreign language well enough for one's interlocutor to recognize one's statements and get the message is usually sufficient for successful communication, even if the statements are not fully grammatically correct. To some extent, this also applies to writing – the key point is to formulate the thoughts in such a way that they can be understood. Minor grammatical mistakes usually do not obstruct the achievement of this goal.

Teaching DHH students to speak in a foreign language is a practice fraught with controversy. Some teachers suggest that, as it is not possible for DHH students to listen freely to foreign speech, they should not be expected to learn to speak the language. Others prove that even if listening is not ideal for them, they may learn how to pronounce foreign speech and lipread it and participate quite effectively in oral communication. The second position is nowadays prevailing as more and more DHH persons actually speak in the majority spoken language and thus want to speak in foreign languages.

The most controversial issue when teaching DHH students to speak in a foreign language is the level of their pronunciation performance and establishing appropriate rules and benchmarks for it. The basis for these benchmarks should be a precise observation and diagnosis of the student's pronunciation skills in his or her national spoken language, so that the aim can be to achieve such a level of pronunciation accuracy as might be achieved by DHH users of that language (cf. Domagała-Zyśk, 2013b).

Speech intelligibility has been defined as "that aspect of speech-language output that allows a listener to understand what a speaker is saying" (Nicolosi, Harryman, & Kresheck, 1996). The speech intelligibility of DHH persons is a dynamic phenomenon, changing throughout their life. It may rise when speech is regularly used and correct pronunciation consciously practised, and it may deteriorate when they are discouraged from using speech in communication, afraid of making mistakes, or worried about not being understood. The level of DHH people's speech intelligibility also depends on social context. It is more intelligible for people familiar with the DHH person's style of pronunciation, and in emotionally supportive and accepting environments with good acoustic conditions. Contemporary research on DHH speech pronunciation also deals with assessing proper articulation of single phonemes, syllables, and words, as well as breath control, speech rate, voice quality, and pitch. Research shows that DHH children learn the phonemes in the same order as hearing children, but this process usually takes longer (Blamey, 2003) and some delays in speech recognition and production are reported. However, this depends on their level of intelligence, level of hearing loss, family background, scope and type of educational and reading experiences, and other school-related factors.

The quality of speech of DHH persons varies according to individual characteristics, but some common features can be observed. The most characteristic factor is centralization of the pronunciation of vocal segments, which means that high vowels are pronounced lower, and low vowels higher. For the listener, it may mean that the majority of vowels sound similar to the neutral vowel schwa (Tye-Murray, 1991). As for consonants, they are usually easier to pronounce, but there are still some difficulties (Levitt & Stromberg, 1983), including incorrect pronunciation of sibilants; problems with sonority; replacing /k/ and /g/ with /x/, and /r/ with /w/; changes in the place of articulation, elisions, affricatives /tʃ/ and /d /: are realized as one element only, with a weak plosive element. The quality of speech and intelligibility do not depend only on the correct pronunciation of single phonemes or syllables, but also on prosodic features such as stress, rhythm, and intonation (Ertmer, 2010).

Typical problems for DHH students in speaking English are described in Domagała-Zyśk (2013b), in which speech therapists of Polish and teachers of English were asked to assess the intelligibility and language production of DHH students in Polish and English. By analyzing the speaking profiles of her six students out of 35 participating in the study did not want to speak in English, and these were the individuals who only rarely spoke in their national language. The other 29 students spoke English, with varying levels of intelligibility. Ten of them were able to use only simple one- or two-word phrases, mainly during classroom conversations; 13 used more complicated English and spoke it both in and out of the classroom; and six were able to speak English freely whether traveling or studying abroad, and in everyday or professional situations. In each case their level of intelligibility in English was similar to or only a bit lower than in their national spoken language.

The six basic difficulties of Polish DHH students learning EFL are summarized by Domagała-Zyśk (2013b) as:

- pronouncing letters and words as they are written, without applying pronunciation rules and habits;
- using sounds from their national spoken language instead of English sounds, for example, using /s/ or /f/ instead of English /th/;
- adding unnecessary sounds where a consonant cluster appears (like in the word *table*);
- not pronouncing /s/ at the end of words in the plural or 3rd person singular forms;
- pronouncing the past tense ending /-ed/ in the same way for all words, without differentiating it into its three different pronunciations; and
- using incorrect stress, rhythm, and intonation patterns.

Numerous strategies have been devised to support DHH students' English pronunciation. Visual Phonics and cued speech are among the most common ones. They possess some similarities: they are used at educational institutions to support national language learning, and though they use gestures, they are not signing systems. Visual Phonics is a system of 46 hand cues which can be used in conjunction with spoken language while teaching reading to primary school students. Its aim is to augment auditory information and make it possible for DHH students to perceive English phonemes in a multisensory way – auditory, visual, tactile, and kinesthetic (Waddy-Smith & Wilson, 2003). The method is used to teach the English reading curriculum in countries where English is a national language, and the results are promising, which supports the conviction that skilled DHH readers use phonological information in word recognition (Schirmer & McGough, 2005). Visual Phonics has not been used yet in Central Europe to teach EFL, though it might be a useful tool for introducing English pronunciation to younger learners. It would be possible only if the teachers learn the system proficiently and the children have thorough access to English classes – which seems to be difficult if they regularly have only 90 minutes of English instruction a week.

Cued speech is another visual communication system that is used to support DHH students with lip-reading and speech recognition and production. The English version of the system consists of eight handshapes produced in four positions near the mouth. Cued speech is used mainly by speech therapists, teachers, and parents to facilitate everyday communication and convey language as precisely as possible. It has been adapted for other languages (e.g. the Polish version of cued speech is named *fonogesty*) which makes cued speech a popular resource for foreign language teaching, especially in cases of migration. British cued speech has been successfully used in Poland by Podlewska (2013, 2016) to teach EFL.

DHH learners' motivation and willingness to speak in English

Willingness to communicate may be defined as "readiness to enter into discourse at a particular time with a specific person or persons, using a L2" (MacIntyre, Clément, Dornyei, & Noels, 1998, p. 547), but is also characterized as a psychological readiness to use a second language, which is not the same as objective competence. We may well imagine a student with objectively good language competence and a weak motivation to use a foreign language, which results in him not using the language in public, versus a student with low competence but strong motivation, who communicates eagerly in the target language. Willingness to communicate may even be treated as a primary goal of learning a foreign language. It can be affected by multiple factors, like self-confidence, interpersonal motivation, group motivation, attitudes, communicative competence, inter-group climate, and personality traits (cf. MacDonald, Clément, & MacIntyre, 2012).

Willingness to communicate in English as a foreign language was studied by Domagała-Zyśk (2013b). She did her research with a group of 15
DHH participants at a workshop called 'English as a tool of international
communication', conducted at the Center of Education of the Deaf and
Hard of Hearing at KUL University in Lublin. This workshop was part of a
program called 'Network of Expert Centers Providing Inclusion in Tertiary
Education'. The mean period of time that they had been learning English
was 6.7 years. The research method included a questionnaire checking the
students' willingness to communicate, the 'Willingness to Communicate
Scale' (McCroskey, 1992), which was translated from English into Polish
by the researcher. Their task was to assess to what extent they felt able
to perform a certain activity: having a small group conversation, giving a
presentation in English, and using English in small groups or large meet-
ings. The results were analyzed statistically and suggested a high level of
willingness to communicate among DHH students – they felt sure that they
could give a presentation in English to a group of friends or acquaintances,
or even strangers. They also felt competent enough to have a conversation
in English with friends or in a small group, though they did not feel confident enough to give a presentation in English to a large unknown audience.

Many DHH students seem to want to speak in a foreign language and
often have the necessary abilities to do this. Domagała-Zyśk and Podlewska
(2012) performed an experiment to investigate this. They collected eight
recordings of reading exercises from prelingually DHH students and asked
native English speakers to assess whether these speech samples could be
regarded as intelligible and correct in terms of pronunciation. The results
showed that on average, the native speakers understood 62% of the content, regarding 52% of it as correctly pronounced. Some individual students
achieved much higher marks: one student scored as high as 81% for intelligibility and 66% for correct pronunciation. It is worth mentioning that
the intelligibility scores here are even higher than in other similar studies.
The intelligibility of DHH students in Osberger, Robbins, Todd, and Riley's
research (1994, in: Blamey, 2003) was assessed at 48%. These results show
that DHH EFL learners are able to master foreign language pronunciation to
such an extent as to be able to be understood by the users of the target language, which is commonly regarded as a primary aim of second language
classes.

Motivation to learn and to speak in a foreign language is an important factor in successful acquisition. This phenomenon has been thoroughly examined by Domagała-Zyśk (2011b), who worked with a group of eleven DHH
university students to assess their motivation to learn English using the
'Motivation to Learn English Scale' created by the researcher (Domagała-
Zyśk, 2011b). Ten of the eleven participants admitted that their main goal in
learning EFL is to be able to communicate with people from other countries.

Pronunciation at work

DHH students in Poland have had the option of learning foreign languages in integrated and mainstream schools since the last decades of the 20th century, but quite often the students have been permitted to focus only on reading and writing, not speaking. Foreign language education started to be offered widely to DHH students in Poland after the 2001 change of state regulations. The new regulations stipulated that all DHH students should receive foreign language instruction at each level of education, and it should be adjusted to their needs. English courses for DHH learners at the John Paul II Catholic University of Lublin began in 2000, and since then, more than 40 students have benefited from them. Straight from the very beginning, the students were encouraged to practise all four language skills: reading and writing, and also – to the greatest possible extent – listening and speaking.

Building on speech therapy habits

One advantage that DHH EFL learners have is their experience of speech therapy classes. They usually start attending them early in their childhood and practise for long hours to achieve correct pronunciation habits in their national spoken language. They possess a high level of knowledge of speech production rules, for example, jaw and lip configurations and tongue movements. As they are used to exercising these, they can quite easily practise new sounds in English, if only given instruction on how to do this. Here are some examples of using speech therapy design to practise EFL:

- Students need instruction on the three different ways of pronouncing the – *ed* suffix. Then in order to practise it, first of all they need to recognize whether the phoneme preceding the ending is voiced or voiceless. Students may need to touch their larynx with a hand while pronouncing the last sound of the word. If they feel the vocal cords vibrating, they know they should use the voiced form of the ending /d/; if they recognize the sound as a voiceless one, they know they are expected to use a voiceless /t/.
- It is difficult for the students to pronounce voiced and voiceless /th/, and often instead use their Polish equivalents /z/, /s/, /d/, or /f/. The teacher may then explain that: if we want to pronounce a voiced /th/, we put the tongue flat between the lower and upper teeth. Then, – holding the tongue tight to the upper teeth, we try to speak the Polish sound /z/.
- If we want to pronounce a voiceless /th/, we follow the same technique as when pronouncing a voiced /th/ but while trying to pronounce the Polish sound /s/. Speech therapists tend to use graphs and arrows to show pronunciation rules; teachers may also use graphs and arrows

to help students practise rising and falling intonation, for example, in sentences like *Isn't she?, Do they?*

• Mirrors are frequently used during speech therapy classes. Using them during English classes and encouraging the students to practise with them at home, reminds students of their speech therapy habits and provides an extra impetus for self-study.

Visually Supported Listening

It is sometimes thought that DHH people are not able to listen to or produce speech, either in the national language or a foreign one. However, nowadays it is rare that DHH individuals do not hear anything. With digital hearing aids and cochlear implants, it is possible for them to notice speech which could not have been heard by DHH people a decade ago.

This knowledge is essential when we plan our classes, as it is not necessary to omit listening exercises and audio materials – instead, we can use the strategy of *Visually Supported Listening*. The basic thing is to discuss with the student the extent to which listening exercises can be used during the classes. Even if it is not possible for the student to follow such exercises in large classrooms, it might be possible to use them while practising English at home or during a tutorial in a quiet room with good acoustics.

If the student is reluctant or unable to follow listening material, we should of course try to make up for this with other types of exercises, like additional reading exercises or using transcripts as reading material. It is worth noting that using a tape script alone may be much less effective than using the recorded material, as all the contextual clues are missing, like the emotional aspects, intonation, and background noises. The same sentence, for example, *Is it beautiful?* can be delivered in many different ways, thus affecting the overall meaning. It sometimes happens that questions checking text comprehension are based on contextual clues; it is then necessary to try to convey the meaning of the text by other methods, like reading the fragment aloud with expressions and intonation suggesting, for example, despair, disgust, or excitement, or to modify the text comprehension question so as to make it possible for the students to answer it without knowing the details that are only discernible through the inaccessible contextual clues.

Practising lip-reading

In listening exercises, lip-reading (i.e. speech-reading) plays a crucial role. It allows them not only to follow the speech more easily, but also to boost their self-esteem and motivation. Speech-reading is possible both in class discussions and while using films (cf. Podlewska, 2021, this volume). In classroom discourse, the interlocutor (either the teacher or another child) should remember the rules of good communication to maximize the utility of lip-reading:

- The speakers' faces should be well lit.
- The speaker should have his or her face directed towards the lip-reader and be close to him/her (but without encroaching on his or her personal space).
- The speaker should not speak too fast or too slowly.
- The pronunciation should be natural, not exaggerated.
- If necessary, the speaker should be ready to repeat things and/or use different language (e.g. a synonym which might be easier to understand).

Video materials including people talking in such a way that their faces and lips are easily read are immensely valuable here. These may be existing materials or can be prepared by the teacher or the students themselves, who may want to record simple everyday situations for the purposes of learning.

Lip-reading can be extensively used in class, depending on the students' abilities; they may be able to lip-read single words, short sentences, or long extracts of foreign speech. Therefore, teachers may want to invite learners to lip-read in various situations, such as while giving instructions (e.g. *Read and answer the questions; First of all, read the text and then answer this question: 'Would you behave similarly to Adeli?'*)

While practising lip-reading in a foreign language, it is usually necessary to support it with imitation, facial expressions, gestures, and writing, and to follow certain rules: 1. One person speaks at a time; 2. If the instruction involves reading, remember that the student cannot do these two activities at the same time. He should first look at you and then read the instruction, or first read the instruction and then look at you and lip-read the question; and 3. Speak clearly and be careful not to rush.

Pronunciation

The reader may have noticed earlier in this chapter that the author tries to take a "golden mean" perspective: point to DHH students' extant skills, but at the same time describe the challenges and the need for individualization. The same applies to pronunciation. Teaching practice shows that there are many DHH students who are able to follow regular English pronunciation and learn it almost perfectly. At the same time, there are those who do not hear the correct way of pronouncing foreign speech, have not yet developed sufficient speech control, and consequently find it difficult to pronounce sounds, words, and sentences correctly enough to be understood by others. The golden mean principle would allow for challenging the learning outcomes of the first group, correcting their pronunciation errors, and teaching the schemata of proper pronunciation as often as possible. The second group may want to learn correct pronunciation of some widely used phrases and use them while in need, but will not be willing or able to reach any kind of meaningful success with foreign language pronunciation. Their situation may be similar to DHH native speakers, who also quite often pronounce speech sounds and phrases incorrectly, but still use speech as one of their means of communication. Citing once again Professor Marek's statement quoted in the introduction to this chapter that we do not possess a right to forbid anybody to speak in any language, the key issue will be how to achieve a level of speech intelligibility that is adequate for communication. It is worth remembering that intelligibility is not a stable measure; it changes with time and practice varies among listeners. The level of speech understanding of people who meet often and/or are used to non-standard speech will usually be higher (Domagała-Zyśk, 2013a).

When practising pronunciation, the International Phonetic Alphabet (IPA) can be helpful, as it enables visualization of the speech sounds. It is commonly used in dictionaries to indicate the pronunciation of words and by non-native learners of English. The first step in using it with DHH students is to teach them the phonetic symbols and try to practise it multi-modally, using all the senses. This may include touching the larynx while pronouncing the sound; connecting the visual symbol of the sound with a certain picture, for example, a picture related to a word in which the sound is clearly distinguished (for i: it might be a picture of a tree;); and trying to pronounce it with the guidance of a teacher or speech therapist. Using IPA symbols, the students can also practise correct speech outside the classroom and independently control their pronunciation. The IPA can help learners to correctly pronounce words with difficult or non-intuitive spelling, like *daughter*, *laughter*, or *neighbour*.

Speech visualization methods

In deaf education, various methods of speech visualization are used to make it easier to 'see' the sounds. One of them is cued speech, which is analyzed in the context of foreign language learning by Anna Podlewska in this volume (cf. also Krakowiak, Domagała-Zyśk, & Podlewska, 2012).

Nowadays, speech can be visualized with the use of technology. It happens systematically when subtitling is provided, either pre-recorded or through a simultaneous service, such as for news programs and theater performances. During university lectures, speech-to-text transliteration helps to provide access to the spoken content. Technology also allows for video calls in which the speaker's face stays visible, enabling lip-reading. Using a mobile phone, one can also text or ask the interlocutor to write down the speech fragments which are not understandable.

Most EFL teachers who work with DHH students visualize speech through imitation, facial expressions, clear pronunciation patterns, slowing down the rate of speech, and making the sounds visible on the lips. Sometimes it is also beneficial to use sign language or fingerspelling, notwithstanding the irregularity of English pronunciation, which can make it tricky to draw parallels between speech and fingerspelling. My students quite often complain that one of the most difficult things in English is that "something is written down and something else completely should be pronounced"; the sounds do not always correspond to the letters, and this is especially so for vowels.

- We write *live* and *like* but say /liv/ and /laik/.
- We write *great* and *greet* but say /greit/ and /gri:t/.

Consequently, the letter *e* can be pronounced in several different ways:

> *shed* /e/, *be* /i:/, *pretty* /i/, *sergeant* /a/, and *café* /ei/.

In order to help my students, I suggested using a couple of hand gestures to visualize the most prominent differences. The most common of them seems to be a two-part gesture suggesting the sound /ai/. This is useful when a student is going to pronounce a word like *hive*, *site*, *try*, *pie*, or *giant*, or when I want to correct his or her pronunciation. The gesture begins with a fist (the 'A' hand shape in sign language linguistics), and then flicks it open. I tried other gestures, but this one seems to work best – it reminds students of the mouth shape we make while pronouncing /ai/ and suggests that they must not close but rather open their mouths (cf. also Sutton-Spence & Boyes Braem, 2001).

Sometimes, even if the spelling suggests differently, we simply need to pronounce /ɪ//l/ or /i:/, like in *heat, beat, meet, meat*, and *give*. To give a hint to our students, we can simply use the 'i' sign language handshape.

Conversations with native speakers

One of the most important goals of foreign language learning is to be able to communicate with native speakers. Because of that, it is very motivating and rewarding if – after a period of learning a language – a student is able to communicate not only with his or her teacher or classmates but also with a native speaker. The success of such an exercise depends mainly on the native speaker's sensitivity, as they have to be careful and understanding, even if the quality of the language used is far from ideal. Such conversations are more important the more independent a speaker the DHH person is. To prepare for such talks (which may be organized at a school or university, or may happen incidentally while DHH students are traveling abroad), the students need to be equipped with some useful strategies for maintaining the conversation, for example, repeating themselves and asking for repetition, or asking their interlocutor to speak more slowly and/or to write down difficult words or phrases.

Digital technology

Access to communication in both sign and spoken language has improved rapidly in recent years (Archbold, 2015). Multimedia has never been so accessible for those with auditory challenges: websites created according to the Web Content Accessibility Guidelines (WCAG, www.w3.org/TR/WCAG20/) should offer both visual and auditory access to the information. Multimedia instruction for DHH students may create an opportunity in the EFL field. This is mainly because it can offer much more visual input than traditional didactic tools: electronic and online dictionaries are often accompanied by pictures or short films that support the understanding and correct usage of new vocabulary. Multimedia also enhances auditory reception, which is important because a vast majority of DHH students do hear to some extent, often with the support of hearing aids (HAs), CIs, and other devices that cooperate with HAs and CIs, like induction loops and FM systems. In this way, they may receive sound of such a good quality that they can recognize, follow, and learn to use foreign speech. Pedagogical practice confirms that for hearing students, multimodality in learning (e.g. a combination of auditory and visual information) is much more fruitful than using only one type of resource (e.g. visual). Such a combination may also be beneficial for many DHH learners who use HAs and CIs (Knoors & Marschark, 2014, p. 214).

There is no other way to learn to speak, than to speak

The majority of DHH people nowadays are able to communicate orally, albeit to varying extents, so there is no reason why they should not speak in other languages than their national one.

Speaking in a foreign language may begin with repeating simple words and phrases, supported with pictures or written text. Then, we can continue with short questions and answers, beginning with general yes/no questions, for example, *Do you like tea?, Have you ever been to Greece?, Are you going to play tennis this weekend?* Another valuable way to practise speech is reading simple dialogues aloud. Even if at the beginning the pronunciation is far from ideal, written material can help the student and teacher to understand each other.

Such exercises let the students feel safe, get accustomed to hearing their voice speak a foreign language, and quite often motivate them to learn more diligently. Only after such simple tasks can we extend the speech exercises to longer sentences, dialogues, and presentations (e.g. a one-minute talk on the student's favorite animal), taking into account their learning level and abilities.

Conclusion

The aim of this chapter was to present some key issues related to the speech and pronunciation of DHH learners. In the first part of the paper, typical problems and barriers were presented, and in the second part, some practical strategies were described.

There are two key aspects to consider when teaching DHH students to speak a foreign language: their physical ability to use speech, which is directly connected with their speech rehabilitation and successes in their national language, and their motivation and willingness to learn to speak in a foreign language. Willingness to communicate should be treated as one of the major factors facilitating the process of learning foreign languages for DHH students. Both language teachers and administrators should pay attention to this characteristic among students and organize a supportive communication environment for students to practise their language competence and keep motivation high.

This supportive environment may include strategies mentioned in this text, like consciously building new speaking skills on the learners' existing speech therapy habits and adjusting the listening exercises to make them approachable for each person individually, so as to respect their intellect and motivation but also their specific learning needs. Lip-reading is of an immense value during foreign language classes, but we should remember DHH persons differ in their mastery of this and even the best lip-readers can catch no more than 30% of what is said. Fortunately, when combined with the use of hearing aids, speech recognition may rise to 80–90% in the listener's national language. In order to achieve good results in speech and pronunciation, DHH learners should be encouraged to speak a foreign language, including with native speakers. In the teaching process, many visual elements should be employed.

The population of DHH learners has been changing and due to digital hearing aids, cochlear implants, and widespread motivation to speak, these students want not only to learn to read and write a foreign language but also to listen to it and speak it. Modern English teachers should facilitate this process as effectively as possible, using strategies that suit the individual learner.

References

Archbold, S. (2015). Being a deaf student. Changes in characteristics and needs. In H. Knoors & M. Marschark (Eds.), *Educating deaf learners* (pp. 23–46). Oxford: Oxford University Press.

Bajko, A., & Kontra, E. (2008). Deaf EFL learners outside the school system. In J. Kormos & E. H. Kontra (Eds.), *Language learners with special needs: An international perspective* (pp. 189–213). Clevedon: Multilingual Matters.

Bajko A., Kontra E. (2008). Deaf EFL learners outside the school system. In: J. Kormos, E.H. Kontra (Eds.), *Language learners with special needs*. Clevedon: Multilingual Matters.

Blamey P.J. (2003). Development of spoken language by deaf children. In: M. Marschark, P.E. Spencer (Eds.), *Deaf Studies, language and education* (pp. 232–246). Oxford: Oxford University Press.

Domagała-Zyśk, E. (2003a). Czy istnieje już surdoglottodydaktyka? *Języki Obce w Szkole*, 4,3–6.

Domagała-Zyśk, E. (2003b). Czy istnieje już surdoglottodydaktyka? *Języki Obce w Szkole*, 4,3–6.

Domagała-Zyśk, E. (2012a). *Poziom motywacji niesłyszących studentów w zakresie uczenia się języków obcych*. W: Kutek-Składek *Student z niepełnosprawnością w środowisku akademickim*. Wydawnictwo Sw. Stanisława BM, s.173–200.

Domagała-Zyśk, E. (2012b). Poziom motywacji niesłyszących studentów do uczenia się języków obcych. In K. Kutek-Sładek, G. Godawa, & Ł. Ryszka (Eds.), *Student z niepełnosprawnością w środowisku akademickim* (pp. 173–200). Kraków: Wydawnictwo św Stanisława BM.

Domagała-Zyśk, E. (2013a). Using technology to teach English as a foreign language to the deaf and hard of hearing. In E. Vilar Beltran, C. Abbott, & J. Jones (Eds.), *Inclusive language education and digital technology* (pp. 84–102). Bristol, London, & Toronto: Multilingual Matters.

Domagała-Zyśk, E. (2013b). Willingness to communicate in English as a foreign language of the deaf and hard of hearing university students. In *Proceedings of the conference universal learning design, Brno 2013* (pp. 65–71). Brno: Masaryk University. ISSN 1805–3947.

Domagała-Zyśk, E., & Podlewska, A. (2012). Umiejętności polskich studentów z uszkodzeniami słuchu w zakresie posługiwania się mówioną formą języka angielskiego. In K. Kutek-Składek (Ed.), *Student z niepełnosprawnością w środowisku akademickim* (pp. 134–157). Kraków: Wydawnictwo Sw Stanisława BM.

Ertmer, D. J. (2010). Relationships between speech intelligibility and word articulation scores in children with hearing loss. *Journal of Speech Language and Hearing Research, 53*(5), 1075–1086. https://doi.org/10.1044/1092-4388(2010/09-0250).

Janakova, D. (Ed.) (2005). *Proceedings 2000. Teaching English to Deaf and hard of Hearing students at secondary and tertiary levels of education in the Czech Republic*. Prague: Eurolex Bohemia.

Knoors, H., & Marschark, M. (Eds.). (2014). *Teaching deaf learners*. Oxford: Oxford University Press.

Kontra, E. H. (2013). Language learning against the odds: retrospective accounts by four Deaf adults. In E. Domagala-Zysk (Ed.), *English as a foreign language for deaf and hard of hearing persons in Europe – state of the art and future challenges* (pp. 93–111). Lublin: Wydawnictwo KUL.

Krakowiak, K., Domagała-Zyśk, E., & Podlewska, A. (2012). Cued speech – A tool to enhance development, education and full family life. In E. Domagała-Zyśk, D. Bis, & A. Rynio (Eds.), *Social and educational support in life-long human development* (pp. 141–160). Lublin: Wydawnictwo KUL.

Levitt, H., & Stromberg, H. (1983). Segmented characteristics of the speech of hearing-impaired children: Factors affecting intelligibility. In: Hochberg I, Levitt

H, Osberger MJ, editors. *Speech of the hearing impaired: Research, training, and personnel preparation* (pp. 53–74). Baltimore: University Park.

MacDonald, J. R., Clément, R., & MacIntyre, P. D. (2003). Willingness to communicate in a L2 in a bilingual context: A qualitative Investigation of Anglophone and Francophone students. Unpublished Manuscript. Retrieved from http:// faculty.cbu.ca/pmacintyre/research_pages/publications.htm

MacIntyre, P. D., Clément, R., Dornyei, Z., & Noels, K. A. (1998). Conceptualizing willingness to communicate in a L2: A situational model of L2 confidence and affiliation. *The Modern Language Journal*, *82*(4), 545–562.

Marschark, M., & Spencer, P. E. (2006). Spoken Language Development of Deaf and Hard-of-Hearing Children: Historical and Theoretical Perspectives. In P. E. Spencer & M. Marschark (Eds.), *Perspectives on deafness. Advances in the spoken language development of deaf and hard-of-hearing children* (pp. 3–21). Oxford University Press.

McCroskey, J. C. (1992). Reliability and validity of the willingness to communicate scale. C*ommunication Quarterly*, *40*, 16–25.

Nicolosi, L., Harryman, E., & Kresheck, J. (1996). *Terminology of communication disorders*. Baltimore: Williams and Wilkins.

Osberger, M. J., Robbins, A. M., Todd, S. L., Riley, A. I., & Miyamoto, R. T. (1994). Speech production skills in children with multichannel cochlear implants. In: Hochmair-Desoyer IJ, Hochmair ES (Eds.), *Advances in cochlear implants* (pp. 503–508). Manz, Vienna: Datenkonvertierung, Reproduktion und Druck.

Podlewska, A. (2013). Cued speech as an empirically-based approach to teaching English as a foreign language to hard of hearing students. In E. Domagała-Zyśk (Ed.), *English as a foreign language for deaf and hard of hearing persons in Europe* (pp. 181–196). Lublin: Wydawnictwo KUL.

Podlewska, A. (2016). The use of cued speech to support the development of verbal language skills in English language instruction for deaf and hard-of-hearing students. In E. Domagała-Zyśk & E. H. Kontra (Eds.), *English as a foreign language for deaf and hard-of-hearing persons: Challenges and strategies* (pp. 23–40). Newcastle upon Tyne: Cambridge Scholars Publishing.

Podlewska, A. (2021). Bringing film to English as a foreign language for the deaf and hard of hearing class. In: E. Domagała-Zyśk, N. Moritz, A. Podlewska (Eds.), *English as a foreign language for deaf and hard of hearing learners* (pp. 54–77). Routledge.

Schirmer, B. R., & McGough, S. M. (2005). Teaching reading to children who are deaf: Do the conclusions of the National Reading Panel apply? *Review of Educational Research*, *75*, 83–117.

Sutherland, I. M. (2008). Everybody wins: Teaching deaf and hard of hearing students together. In T. Berberi, E. C. Hamilton, & I. M. Sutherland (Eds.), *Worlds apart? Disability and foreign language learning* (pp. 42–69). New Haven, CT & London: Yale University Press.

Sutton-Spence, P., & Boyes Braem, R. L. (2001). *The hands are the head of the mouth: The mouth as articulator in sign languages*. Hamburg: Signum Press.

Tye-Murray, N. (1991). The establishment of open articulatory postures by deaf and hearing talkers. *Journal of Speech and Hearing Research*, *34*, 453–459.

Waddy-Smith, B., & Wilson, V. (2003). See that sound! Visual phonics helps deaf and hard of hearing students develop reading skills. *Odyssey*, *5*, 14–17.

2 Phonic reading as a strategy in learning to read English as a foreign language for deaf and hard of hearing pupils

Patricia Pritchard

Introduction

This chapter first outlines the challenges that young DHH pupils face when learning to read EFL. Then the focus turns to decoding English texts using phonic reading. Good readers make use of many different strategies to decode written text to promote comprehension. Research shows an important factor is having knowledge of the foreign language's speech sounds and how they are represented in writing. Developing phonological awareness is a necessary and fundamental part of learning to read, regardless of the degree of hearing loss, but demands an explicit teaching approach tailored to the individual. Studies show that many DHH children acquire letter-sound correspondence and use multi-sensory information to create phonological representations that are not purely auditory. A survey of a small, random group of Norwegian DHH pupils from several mainstream 4th grade classes revealed they had little knowledge of English speech sounds and spelling patterns. The chapter outlines the teaching that helped these pupils to develop phonic reading, which involved all the senses.

This chapter was initially motivated by an informal assessment that was carried out as part of preparation for an EFL teaching session. The results of that assessment gave rise to concerns that will be outlined. To provide some background, it is necessary to mention that in Norway, 95% of deaf children are fitted with cochlear implants (CIs), although there is a marked variation in outcomes. The widespread use of CIs and the improvements in hearing aid technology have given children with serious hearing losses the opportunity to make more use of their residual hearing. This has led to mainstreaming in Norway and the closure of all state-run schools for the deaf. However, DHH pupils are offered regular short-term stays, usually consisting of 6 weeks during each school year, at state-run regional resource centres in a sign language environment. DHH pupils can start to learn English in the 1st grade.

The chapter aims to give teachers *research-based guidance* on how to develop their practice when working with young DHH learners of EFL. The focus of this chapter is on a reading strategy that can enable young Norwegian DHH pupils to decode English written words through phonic reading. However, phonic reading is only one of several strategies needed to read and comprehend meaning. The ability to comprehend the meaning of a text demands competence in many areas, and skills in decoding the written word play only a part.

Reading English as a foreign language and DHH pupils

Reading is a complex skill that must be learnt and is often broadly described as consisting of two main activities: decoding and comprehension (Easterbrooks & Beal-Alvarez, 2013, p. 117). Unlike sign language, English speech and written language is based on sound in a linear fashion. There are many ways of decoding written words. For example, the reader can simply remember what a word looks like, but unfortunately, there is a limit to how many words one can memorise, and that limit is too low to make the reader fluent. Alternatively, the reader can take words apart and put them back together again: either sound by sound; morpheme by morpheme (such as a word's root and affixes); or visually, letter by letter, spelling-pattern by spelling-pattern. Some of these strategies are more effective than others, therefore there is a need for explicit, systematic teaching. Also, as individuals we have different preferences and learning styles, so pupils need to experience many different strategies to be able to find out which ones suit them best.

It is important to note that decoding is not enough in itself, as the main purpose of reading is comprehension. Comprehension consists of understanding the meaning of words in context and, ultimately, the author's message, purpose, perspective, and attitude.

English written language is based on spoken English that consists of speech sounds, which means that phonological awareness (PA) is vital. PA occurs when the learner realizes that words are made up of a certain number of speech sounds known as phonemes and can recognise them. Research has been equivocal about the importance of PA in the development of DHH children's reading skills (Harris & Beech, 1998; Dyer, MacSweeney, Szczerbinski, & Green, 2003). In hearing children, PA is seen as essential and develops through listening to and experimenting with spoken language. Experience shows that developing PA is also a necessary part of learning to read for DHH pupils, regardless of the degree of hearing loss, but obviously demands an appropriate approach including the visual and tactile senses, and explicit teaching tailored to each individual. Many DHH children with severe hearing losses are able to acquire letter-sound correspondences (East-erbrooks & Beal-Alvarez, 2013, p. 217), and this is necessary whether they are learning to read Norwegian (L1) or English as a foreign language (L2).

Moreover, August and Shanahan (2006) showed in their research that an important factor in decoding and reading a foreign language is knowledge of that language's speech sounds and how they are represented in writing. This factor is embedded in both the former (2013) and the new Norwegian National Curriculum in English for Pupils with Sign Language (Utdan-ningsdirektoratet, 2020). The new curriculum states that by the end of 2nd grade, DHH pupils aged eight should be able to: "Experiment with and use basis mouth patterns, speech sound and syllables. Connect speech sounds to letters and spelling patterns and blend letters' sounds into words" (Author's translation).

Experience shows that pupils naturally transfer skills used in reading Norwegian to the task of learning to read English, although in English there is not always such a clear one-to-one correspondence between speech sounds and letters as there is in Norwegian. This means that new reading skills must be learned to read English texts.

Why is English important and what makes learning EFL challenging for deaf and hard of hearing pupils?

Across all aspects of life today, including education, private life, and work, skills in English are vitally important to function in our globalized world. Pupils with hearing loss, like everyone else, have expectations of becoming active, contributing citizens in society. However, they may often find that learning spoken language can be a challenge, along with learning to read and write. Nonetheless, language development usually follows a normal pattern in DHH children exposed early to sign language, and they readily learn other sign languages (Pritchard, 2004). Thus, a hearing loss is not necessarily the cause of difficulties in language learning or learning EFL. There are many factors that can influence a pupil's success. Here are just some of them:

The pupil

- The pupil's motivation and interest in foreign language learning
- The time of onset and when the hearing loss was diagnosed
- The degree and type of hearing loss, which can influence the perception of speech sounds and the ability to differentiate sounds from each other
- The influence the hearing loss has on working memory and auditory memory
- How much and the kind of early education the pupil has experienced

* The pupil's exposure (or lack of exposure) to English and/or British Sign Language[1] (BSL) or American Sign Language (ASL) outside the classroom

The mainstream learning environment

* may not provide adequate access to English in a mode that the DHH pupil can perceive and comprehend
* may provide little access to incidental learning, repetition, conversation, and classroom discussions because of the lack of a common language used by the DHH pupil, fellow pupils, and teachers and may not include the widespread use of the native sign language
* may not provide optimal listening conditions because of large classes, visual distractions, and background noise
* may not provide teaching based on the DHH pupil's needs
* may not facilitate or ensure the effective use of technical aids

It is worth noting that a recent Norwegian survey revealed that few DHH students perceive the overall communication in their mainstream classrooms at an optimal level. Their biggest problem is hearing their fellow students (Rekkedal, 2017).

Teaching EFL to DHH pupils in mainstream classrooms makes certain demands on teachers, which give rise to several questions:

* Do teachers have the necessary competence and training to teach DHH pupils, and do they have sufficient insight into pupils' many varying needs?
* Is the chosen teaching approach appropriate for the DHH pupil? Has the teacher made suitable adaptions or is it left to the pupil to take responsibility for adapting to the current teaching practice (Kermit, 2018)?
* Is there a mismatch between the DHH pupil's and teacher's language mode? In other words, is an oral approach being used when the national sign language and BSL or ASL would be more effective, or vice versa?
* Are teachers relying too much on technical aids and the pupil's ability to speech read?
* Are teachers making regular assessments of the pupil's progress to ensure development, and are assessments used in the adaption and planning of lessons?

Research aims and objectives

If we accept that the knowledge of English speech sounds and how they are represented in writing form part of the basis for decoding text, then it follows that it is important to know whether DHH pupils have this know-how and can use it. As mentioned earlier, this is a learning goal for 2nd graders in the Norwegian National Curriculum in English for the pupils with sign language (Utdanningsdirektoratet. Læreplan i engelsk for elever med tegnspråk, 2020). At the time this assessment was done, the former curriculum was in use and the same goal was then set for 4th graders.

With this in mind, at the beginning of a short-term stay at a regional resource centre, a random group of five DHH 4th grade pupils were assessed on their ability to recognize the written representation of basic English speech sounds. The aim of the assessment was to provide information for the planning of English lessons for the group during their stay.

Instruments and procedure

An assessment test, *Read Aloud*, was created for this purpose as no other appropriate measure was found. *Read Aloud* focuses on English speech sounds that are not found in spoken Norwegian, and letters that have an unfamiliar pronunciation for Norwegians. There are also some common English spelling patterns that are not used in Norwegian and that pupils need to recognize. To meet these requirements, *Read Aloud* encompassed:

- consonants represented by the letters c, j, r, w, y, and z, and the short vowels a, e, i, o, and u
- unfamiliar individual words made up of a consonant, a short vowel, and a consonant (CVC), for example *wig* and *jug*
- unfamiliar short texts made up of CVC words
- the digraphs th, sh, ch, and qu, and the so-called long vowel spelling patterns: ay, ee, igh, ow, and oo
- the 25 most common small words, for example *and, the,* and *I*
- other spelling patterns for the long vowels: -a-e, -e-e, -i-e, -o-e, and -u-e; -ai, -ee, -ei, -oa, and -ue
- unfamiliar phonic texts involving all the previous items

Spelling patterns involving so-called 'Bossy R', such as -ar, -air, -ear, etc., were not assessed. The items were organized with a gradually increasing degree of difficulty. The assessment was carried out with each pupil individually in quiet surroundings. Instructions were given in Norwegian or Norwegian Sign Language (NSL) according to the pupil's preference, and then repeated in Signed English. Pupils could use technical aids and speech reading. They were given some practice items first and all responded in spoken English, sometimes accompanied by BSL fingerspelling.

Participants

The group that was assessed consisted of five mainstreamed pupils in 4th grade. They all used CIs or hearing aids, could read and speak Norwegian, and could use NSL. The pupils were also used to communicating in sign-supported Norwegian and had no additional learning difficulties. With this group, who made use of residual hearing and spoken language, it was appropriate to expect them to read aloud in spoken English. If this had not been the case, another approach would have been used.

Results of the assessment

Unfortunately, the results of the assessment showed that the group could make little use of phonic reading as a strategy to decode text. They had little knowledge of English speech sounds and spelling patterns and seemed to be memorizing English 'word pictures', or sight-reading. While it is advantageous to have a sight-reading vocabulary, this alone is not an effective strategy when dealing with new, unfamiliar words. Some responded using English letter names or Norwegian speech sounds when trying to read unfamiliar English words. There were few correct responses and no apparent patterns as to which, if any, speech sounds had been acquired. Two pupils in the group volunteered to read an unfamiliar phonic text aloud. (A phonic text is one where unfamiliar words can be decoded by sounding out the letter sounds.) Both children read the text quickly, which could give an impression of fluency, but their reading was imprecise, leaving out some sounds and words and sometimes substituting Norwegian speech sounds for English ones. The results are more fully described in an article entitled *Lesing i engelskfaget og hørselshemmede elever* (Reading in English and DHH pupils) (Pritchard, 2018).

The results of this assessment cannot be generalized to apply to the DHH group as a whole, since the test group was extremely small. However, the results give cause for concern and demonstrate the need to re-think teaching strategies. Here we have a group of pupils with the potential to learn EFL who have not been given a foundation for the development of their English literacy skills. Since this was an informal assessment and not a formal study, it is not known which teaching methods the group's teachers used, and whether the teachers had explicitly and systematically taught English speech sounds as part of the teaching of reading in English.

Based upon the assessment, the group was given lessons in phonic reading during their short-term stay. Each speech sound was taught explicitly according to individual needs by giving each an individually adapted work program.

Their teachers were given full reports on which speech sounds needed to be taught to each individual pupil. However, it is not known whether the teachers did any follow-up in their mainstream classrooms.

What can we learn?

Regular assessment is required to ensure several things: that there is no mismatch between the teacher's language mode and the pupil's actual needs, that teaching methods are appropriate, and that learning goals are being reached. Whatever the type or degree of hearing loss, the pupil needs additional sensory support to help him learn and remember new speech sounds, words, and concepts.

Which teaching strategies can we use in developing phonic skills?

The first step is to develop PA in DHH pupils' L1 and then develop these skills in the L2 – in this case English. It is never too early to start playing with and exploring language and developing PA. Because of the challenges DHH pupils face in gaining access to sound, we must make use of all the senses when we teach PA, and we must continue doing so when we teach speech sounds, spelling patterns, and the blending of the sounds into words. Listening alone is not enough and residual hearing by itself cannot provide a clear and reliable input. Fortunately the other senses can be drawn upon to compensate, provide additional experiences, and reinforce input:

- Visual: signs, fingerspelling, mouthings, speech reading, body language, and written letters
- Tactile: perception of movement in the oral cavity when producing speech sounds; detecting vibrations on the face, throat, and chest; and detecting the rhythm of speech with the whole body
- Movement: signs, fingerspelling, Visual Phonics, cued speech, gestures and body movements, writing on different surfaces, clapping syllables, dance, making letters with your whole body, etc.

In this way, DHH pupils can experience success and mastery (Pritchard & Zahl, 2010). This means that by using all the senses, DHH pupils mentally create phonological representations that are not purely based on sound (Leybaert, 1993).

The teacher must be observant and find out which senses a pupil is employing, and then adapt play activities to support PA development. Studies have shown, for example, that some deaf 3-year-olds decode words using fingerspelling and lip movements (Roos, 2009). In a study of Norwegian deaf readers, Arnesen et al. (2002) concluded that most have a form of articulatory decoding, and Roos (2009) suggests that mature readers, both hearing and DHH, exploit PA. It is important to establish an appropriate level of PA through play and games before pupils start to learn letter sounds and blend them together to form words.

For some DHH pupils, it may be difficult or impossible to distinguish between speech sounds, syllables, and words that sound, feel, and look very similar, for example /m/ and /b/ and *ship* and *sheep*. Play activities with speech sounds, syllables, and rhymes should start with examples that contain strong contrasts that are easy to speech read. Pupils can find words with the same number of syllables by clapping the word's rhythm while drawing on their knowledge of NSL where signs often follow the same rhythm as the word they are associated with. We can also have games where we find words that begin with the same sound or have the same sound in the middle or at the end, to develop speech reading skills and PA (Pritchard & Zahl, 2010).

Teachers need to describe sounds and make pupils conscious of tactile and visual clues. There is a need to talk about voiced and unvoiced sounds (/d/ and /t/), visible and invisible articulations (/m/ and /k/), plosives or explosions of air (/ʧ/), nasal sounds (/ŋ/), fricatives (/s/), how sounds are produced, and how speech sounds can and cannot be put together. We also need to explore the properties of consonants and vowels and use colour codes to separate them in writing. We can make use of this later to illustrate spelling patterns.

Developing PA and connecting English speech sounds to letters should be done early in a child's school career and over a relatively short period. As soon as pupils have a grasp of Norwegian (L1) phonic reading, teachers can introduce English phonics (L2). Experience shows that this work usually proceeds quickly at this stage, although for older pupils, intensive short "reading courses" are one way of compensating for lost time.

It is necessary to teach the 44 English speech sounds systematically and explicitly, and pupils need to master the sound attributed to each letter or spelling pattern if they are going to be able to apply this knowledge to decoding text. Some letters in L1 (Norwegian) are associated with the same sound in L1 and L2 (English), and these are quickly dealt with.

We begin with individual letters that have a one-to-one correspondence with a language sound. By focusing on each language sound explicitly and combining written tasks with games utilizing all the senses, pupils quickly acquire the ability to discuss similarities and differences between Norwegian and English. Using phonic information, pupils blend language sounds (voiced or not) and can independently learn new words and phrases through reading.

A complicating factor is that in English, there are more speech sounds than letters in the alphabet. Therefore, pupils must learn spelling patterns which are groups of letters representing one speech sound. Furthermore, pupils require an overview of the most common English spelling patterns to promote an understanding of how the speech sounds are represented in writing. Overviews used in teaching English as an L1 can be useful in EFL, such as those found in Miskin (2016). Another factor that makes written English complicated is that the same speech sound can have several different spelling patterns: for example, /ei/ can be written as *-ay, -a-e, ai, eigh, a, ei, ey*, or *aigh*. This is illustrated well in Miskin's (2016) 'speed sound poster'. Teachers need to have knowledge and understanding of the different spelling patterns and focus on them when working with pupils on decoding or writing a text. Some English spelling patterns are rarely used, for example -que for /k/; therefore, it is wise to teach the most common forms to give pupils a foundation to work from and confidence to read, write, and maybe speak English. This can be done using graded phonic reading books, which give pupils the opportunity to practise and gain confidence in using their new-found phonic reading skills. It is the teacher's responsibility to source phonic texts that are age appropriate. Whether pupils pronounce words and use their voice and intonation correctly is not the main issue; rather, the priority is for them to develop a mental representation of the word and associate it with meaning.

After the basic mechanics are learnt through phonic reading, literacy development is based more on language and thinking skills (metalinguistic and cognitive strategies) that are continuously developing. Importantly, language skills include using knowledge of morphology and syntax.

Teachers can use the 'chaining method', where all the pupils' senses are engaged in language learning (Humphries & MacDougall, 2000). This ensures that the brain receives many different experiences to help it remember new speech sounds and words and understand new concepts. Here is a list of EFL chaining experiences in no particular order:

- Experience an event or see a concrete item, person, or picture.
- See the BSL sign and mouth it.
- Perform the sign that represents an English word.
- Fingerspell individual letters and spelling patterns using the BSL alphabet.
- Fingerspell a word using the BSL alphabet.
- Gain awareness of the tactile feedback from the oral cavity, throat, and face when forming the oral components of a sign or the speech sounds in a word.
- Listen to a spoken word or phrase and repeat it.

- Speech read what is being said.
- Look at the shape of a written word.
- Colour code consonants and vowels in a word to identify spelling patterns.
- Decode a word forming the English speech sounds (not necessarily voiced).
- Sound out, blend the sounds together, and read the word.
- Clap the syllables in a word.
- Deconstruct a word and find the word's root, for example by taking away affixes, to understand the morphology of the word.
- Translate words into NSL and/or spoken and written Norwegian.

To become a fluent reader, the pupil needs the motivation to read frequently, and must also practise using different strategies. Opportunities for repetition and practising English are not always readily available for DHH pupils unless teachers are aware of how to facilitate this. Lacking access to mainstream classroom discussions can also hinder incidental learning and harm the development of the general knowledge and vocabulary needed in reading comprehension. To mitigate this, teachers can use communication games such as 'Non-stop paper switch' or 'Information gap'. They are an effective tool that can improve inclusion and allow pupils to use and experiment with new speech sounds and language.

How teachers approach the reading of a text can influence comprehension. Sometimes it appears that teachers try to do too much at once and pupils become overwhelmed. Re-reading a text with different aims for each reading gives opportunities for more explicit teaching (Charlesworth, Charlesworth, Raban, & Rickars, 2006). First, activating pupils' prior knowledge of the subject of the text is necessary. This means that teachers should check pupils' understanding of the necessary concepts in L1 and add more if necessary. Giving the pupils a short summary of the text in L1, using information from the pictures, titles, and layout, provides pupils with context, creates interest in the text, and enables predictions about the meaning of unfamiliar words and what may happen next.

Thereafter, pupils need a visual summary of the content in English (L2) using pictures, diagrams, BSL or ASL signs, mime, and gestures, before reading the actual text. These activities will aid comprehension of the written text. It is wise to give pupils key words and common words plucked out of the story and to isolate them on flashcards. Key words can then be sounded out, along with any other segments that can be phonically decoded at this stage in pupils' development. Some words will become decodable as pupils learn more and more spelling patterns. Many common small words can be phonically decoded, but it is also advantageous to sight read them.

Lists of the most common English words can be found on the internet. Flashcards can be used in games to provide repetition so that words are recognized automatically.

At the first reading in L2 keep the languages visible: signed and/or spoken and written and focus on decoding the words using various strategies including phonic reading. At the second reading the focus is on finding the meaning of words and phrases using cognitive strategies to aid comprehension (Easterbrooks & Beal-Alvarez, 2013). It is also helpful to ask pupils to reflect on what could have happened before and after the story and what characters can be feeling or thinking.

Finally, pupils can practise reading the text and can present it in a mode that suits their individual abilities and preferences, whether signed or spoken.

To summarize, after the preparatory activities are completed, the aim of the first reading is to decode the text and make use of different strategies, including phonic reading. At the next reading, the aim is to find the meaning and intention of the author. The final reading is a presentation of the text by the pupil in a language mode of his or her choice.

Conclusion

Studies show that PA, and knowledge of English speech sounds and their representation in writing, are important for all children learning to read. Unfortunately, studies show that DHH pupils often have fewer reading strategies compared to their hearing classmates (Strassman, 1997; Marschark & Hauser, 2008). Exposure to English and the implicit development of language understanding is crucial for all young language learners (Dahl, 2015). However, DHH pupils commonly experience lower levels of English input, both inside and outside the classroom, resulting in smaller vocabularies than their classmates'. This can be yet another factor limiting DHH pupils' development of PA, because of the shortage of words available to them that they can analyze and search for patterns. Therefore, there is a need for systematic teaching of many different strategies, of which phonic reading is a basic and important one. For DHH pupils learning EFL this also means developing strategies that take advantage of their multilingualism in signed and spoken languages, which helps them to reflect on how English works and is structured.

Research and personal experience indicate that the learning of English speech sounds using all the senses, regardless of the level of hearing loss and access to sound, is beneficial for DHH pupils reading EFL. With insufficient knowledge of English speech sounds and spelling patterns, pupils may be insecure readers and writers and could be prevented from reaching their full potential. Thus, it would be prudent to put research into practice and reassess the teaching of DHH pupils in the EFL classroom.

Note

1 The use of BSL in teaching EFL is described in *English as a foreign language for deaf and hard of hearing persons in Europe* (2013). The teaching of English to deaf and severely hard of hearing pupils in Norway. P. Pritchard.

References

Arnesen, K., Enerstvedt, R. T., Engen, E. A., Engen, T., Høie, G., & Vonen, A. M. (2002). *Tospråklighet og lesing/skriving hos døve barn. En kartlegging av grunnskoleelever og deres språklige situasjon* [Bilingualism and reading and writing in deaf children. A survey of primary school pupils and their linguistic situation]. Oslo: Skådalen kompetansesenter.

August, D., & Shanahan, T. (Eds.). (2006). *Developing literacy in second-language learners: Report of the national literacy panel on language-minority children and youth. Executive Summary.* Mahwah, New Jersey and London: Lawrence Erlbaum Associates.

Charlesworth, A., Charlesworth, R., Raban, B., & Rickars, F. (2006). Reading recovery for children with hearing loss. *The Volta Review, 106*(1), 29–51.

Dahl, A. (2015). Utvikling av språkforståelse i tidlig start med engelsk [Development of English comprehension during first grade]. *Comunicare, 1*, 4–8. Retrieved November 2018 from www.fremmedspraksenteret.no/

Dyer, A., MacSweeney, M., Szczerbinski, M., & Green, L. (2003). Predictors of reading delay in deaf adolescents: The relative contributions of rapid automatized naming speed and phonological awareness and decoding. *Journal of Deaf Studies and Deaf Education, 8,* 213–229.

Easterbrooks, S. R., & Beal-Alvarez, J. (2013). *Literacy instruction for students who are deaf and hard of hearing.* New York: Oxford University Press.

Harris, M., & Beech, J. R. (1998). Implicit phonological awareness and early reading development in prelingually deaf children. *Journal of Deaf Studies and Deaf Education, 3*(3), 205–216.

Humphries, T., & MacDougall, F. (2000). Chaining and other links: Making connections between American Sign Language and English in two types of school settings. *Visual Anthropology Review, 15*(2), 84–94.

Kermit, P. (2018) *Hørselshemmede barn og unges opplæringsmessige og sosiale vilkår i barnehage og skole – Kunnskapsoversikt over nyere nordisk forskning. Mangfold og inkludering* [Hearing impaired children and young people's educational and social conditions in kindergarten and school – Overview of recent Nordic research. Diversity and inclusion]. Trondheim, Norway: NTNU Samfunnsforskning.

Leybaert, J. (1993). Reading in the deaf: The role of phonological codes. In M. Marschark & M. D. Clark (Eds.), *Psychological perspective on deafness* (pp. 269–310). Mahwah, NJ: Lawrence Erlbaum Associates.

Marschark, M., & Hauser, P. C. (2008). *Deaf cognition: Foundations and outcomes*. New York: Oxford University Press.

Miskin, R. (2016). *Read write inc. phonics: Teaching handbook Vol. 1*. Oxford: Oxford University Press.

Pritchard, P. (2004). TEFL for deaf pupils in Norwegian bilingual schools: Can deaf primary school pupils acquire a foreign sign language? Masters thesis in Special Education. Norwegian University of Science & Technology. Trondheim, Norway.

Pritchard, P. (2018). Lesing i engelskfaget og hørselshemmede elever [Reading in English and DHH pupils]. In *Spesial Pedagogikk* 06/18, 26–33 Oslo: utdanningsforbundet.

Pritchard, P., & Zahl, T. S. (2010). *Veiene til en god bimodal tospråklighet hos døve og sterkt tunghørte* [The roads to a good sign-bilingual development in the deaf and severely hard-of-hearing]. Statped vest. Statped skriftserien nr 86. Oslo: Statped.

Rekkedal, A. M. (2017). Factors associated with school participation among students with hearing loss. *Scandinavian Journal of Disability Research, 19*(3), 175–193.

Roos, C. (2009). *Laslara och skriftspråka før barn med døvehet eller hørselsnedsattning* [Learning to read and write for deaf and hearing-impaired children]. Special pedagogiska skolemyndigheten. Retrieved July 2009 from www.spsm.se

Strassman, B. K. (1997). Metacognition and reading in children who are deaf: A review of the research. *Journal of Deaf Studies and Deaf Education, 2*(3), 140–149.

Utdanningsdirektoratet (2013). *Læreplan i engelsk for hørselshemmede* [National curriculum in English for the hearing-impaired]. Retrieved from Utdanningdirektoratet website www.udir.no/kl06/ENG2-03/Hele/Formaal/

Utdanningsdirektoratet (2020). *Læreplan i engelsk for elever med tegnspråk* [National curriculum in English for pupils with sign language]. Retrieved from Utdanningdirektoratet website 28 September 2020, www.udir.no/lk20/eng02-04

3 Using cartoons as a strategy for enhancing oral communication in EFL classes for deaf and hard of hearing students

Nuzha Moritz

Introduction

The dream of every teacher is to have a dynamic, motivated, and productive classroom. Teaching oral communication to DHH learners successfully can be a challenging task. To enhance oral communication, we should consider one important element, which is necessary for language performance: motivation. Motivation can be intrinsic or extrinsic. Students are likely to be intrinsically motivated if they are interested in mastering a topic and having fun rather than just achieving good marks or results. Students with higher intrinsic motivation are possibly more successful. Intrinsic motivation involves engaging in a positive behavior because it is personally rewarding. It is gratifying to essentially perform an activity for its own sake rather than for some external reward. As shown in the literature, one of the means of enhancing oral communication is by using audio-visual materials like videos, songs, films, documentaries, and cartoons. For instance, using cartoons to teach English to DHH students can make learning enjoyable and effective. Carefully prepared cartoons can increase understanding, add interest to a subject, and increase memory retention. For DHH learners, visual materials like cartoons can elicit interest and build confidence because they are fun, colorful, entertaining, and simple to understand; this can enhance DHH learners' desire to communicate (Katchen, 1995).

Effective methods for teaching EFL

We believe that effectiveness in teaching DHH students could be positively correlated with accommodating learners by exploiting a diversity of approaches and teaching methods in the EFL classroom (Bochner, 1982). Methods and approaches for teaching foreign languages have undergone many changes through the years. The combination of traditional teaching techniques and new technologies has allowed teachers to improve outcomes

(Parasnis, 1997). The learner has also become the center of the teaching and learning process, as EFL teachers have increasingly taken into account the individual differences among learners and sought to enhance the capacities of each student. New pedagogical approaches have brought the use of audio-visual materials among other technical innovations (Hemei 1979). The use of these materials is seen as having broad advantages for all learners as they increase learners' awareness of linguistic diversity and learning strategies as shown by Parasnis (1997, p. 75):

> The need to accommodate a deaf learner's reliance on the visual modality can be viewed as an asset and not a liability, since many hearing learners will also benefit from teaching that effectively utilizes the visual medium in the classroom . . . thus, it can be argued that such accommodation will generally lead to enhanced educational experiences for all learners.

Motivation

Motivation is an essential element not only for learning a foreign language but also in life generally. Motivation can be divided into two categories: intrinsic and extrinsic. If we have a closer look at their definitions, we see that both lead to a sort of satisfaction, but as mentioned, in the context of EFL, the former is usually more effective.

Intrinsic motivation

According to Ryan and Deci (2000, p. 56):

> Intrinsic motivation is defined as the doing of an activity for its inherent satisfaction rather than for some separable consequences. When intrinsically motivated, a person is moved to act for the fun or challenge entailed rather than because of external products, pressures or rewards.

From our experience in EFL teaching, we have noticed that students are likely to be intrinsically motivated in class if they are interested in mastering a topic and having fun rather than just rote learning to achieve good results. In other words, students with high intrinsic motivation possibly have better achievements than students who have low intrinsic motivation. Intrinsic motivation involves engaging in a behavior because it is personally rewarding to essentially perform an activity for its own sake rather than the desire for some external rewards (Ryan & Deci, 2000). Examples of actions that are the result of intrinsic motivation include participating in a sport activity because you find it enjoyable, solving a word puzzle because you find it challenging and fun, and taking part in a competition or game because you find it exciting. In each of these examples, the behavior is motivated by an internal desire to participate in an activity for its own sake. If a student is highly intrinsically motivated and enjoys learning a foreign language, the outcome is more likely to be worthwhile (Ryan & Deci, 2000).

Extrinsic motivation

Extrinsic motivation is defined as

> a construct that pertains whenever an activity is done in order to attain some separable outcome. Extrinsic motivation thus contrasts with intrinsic motivation, which refers to doing an activity simply for the enjoyment of the activity itself, rather than its instrumental value.
>
> (Ryan and Deci, 2000, p. 56)

Extrinsic motivation thus refers to motivation that comes from outside an individual. The motivating factors are external rewards such as money, grades, or avoiding punishment. These factors provide satisfaction, relief, and/or pleasure that the task itself may not provide (Bainbridge, 2015).

In this pilot study, our concern is how we can motivate our students intrinsically to enhance both oral communication and language performance.

The use of cartoons as teaching tools to enhance communication

The media in general play an important role as a teaching aid to achieve learning goals (Wittich & Schuller, 1953). Many researchers have emphasized the positive psychological impacts of using cartoons as classroom materials that provide authentic language input, (Lochrie, 1992) and (Nunan, 1999). Rae (2000) and Gilmore (2007) underscored the notion that cartoons can improve the learning atmosphere, break the monotony, and reduce boredom and stress in a classroom and could even be of great help in teaching grammar. Along the same lines, Clark (2000) emphasized the fact that cartoons can enhance the thinking process and discussion skills. The positive impact of cartoons can be attributed to their humour, simple plots, and exaggerated actions and speech. Doring (2002) provided evidence that students who used cartoons in the classroom could communicate and take part in discussions easily compared to classes using traditional materials. Finally, Rule and Auge (2005) confirmed that the casual atmosphere that is often generated when cartoons are used leads to a high degree of motivation.

The next part focuses on the use of cartoons as a means of promoting intrinsic motivation to enhance oral communication in an EFL class for DHH students and begins by briefly considering some of the advantages and disadvantages of using cartoons in classrooms.

Cartoons: advantages and drawbacks

Animated cartoons have always constituted entertainment for children, but nowadays all age groups tend to watch cartoons. In classrooms, cartoons can be selected according to the learners' ages, language levels, and the lesson objectives. Cartoons generally portray interpretations of situations and stories using a set of animated drawings instead of real places, objects, or actors. It is also true of cartoons that they allow for imagination and enable characters to do impossible things, which contributes to their success (Katchen, 1995).

We might think that cartoons will not work as listening activities in EFL classes because they are sometimes difficult to understand, especially for DHH learners. There are several challenging features for non-native learners when they watch a cartoon in a foreign language, according to Katchen (1995). The first is the fact that there are few clues from visual articulation; in other words, lip-reading is not possible. Lip-reading depends on real movements not only of the lips but also the mouth, teeth, jaw, and tongue, and these subtle movements are completely missing in cartoons since the characters' mouths are made to imitate real people but do not correspond well to actual speech. Exaggerated speech is another challenge, as specific and unusual voice elements are used, like higher voice frequency, lisping, stammering, hesitations, and unnatural-sounding voices. Other paralinguistic features like body language, gestures, facial expressions, etc., are also commonly found in cartoons, as well as regional accents and speech rate, pitch, and fluency, which could be challenging for hard of hearing learners. Cartoon producers also tend to add on altered or unusual voice quality to make characters sound stupid, creepy, distressed, sweet, shy, wise, mean, naughty, helpless, etc. A DHH learner may have little experience with comprehending these unnatural-sounding voices (Katchen, 1995).

Despite these drawbacks, using cartoons in the EFL classroom still has significant advantages. Cartoons have purposive communication, and when carefully chosen they could be a real asset in a classroom (Kemp, 1963, cited in Mustika, 2010).

Using cartoons in class can attract the students' attention and elicit their curiosity because cartoons tend to be colorful, amusing, attractive, entertaining, and simple to understand (Wittich & Schuller, 1953, p. 138). One crucial feature in cartoons is the simplicity of the story line or plot, which most of the time is easy to follow. Comical situations and jokes help to create a relaxed, stimulating class atmosphere and an environment that is conducive to learning. The students will also be exposed to a wide range of language registers, including informal vocabulary and slang. Cartoons can highlight not only language-relevant history and culture but also societal issues like gun control. Many historical and cultural events are featured in cartoons, such as Halloween, Thanksgiving, and St. Patrick's Day (Katchen, 1993). The focus can be adapted according to the language level of the class.

Although the listening input could be a challenge for DHH learners, the visual features offer cognitive experiences and provoke discussion. Apart from the fun and educational aspects of cartoons, they allow action after watching, and encourage learners to take turns as active speakers, thus enhancing their oral communication ability.

Action research: classroom observation experience

The observation was conducted with first year students at the University of Strasbourg in France. The main task was to observe the students' degree of participation in the classroom activities. I adopted the action research approach (Lewin, 1946) which, is based on lesson observation. It is a way to observe our own lessons with the goal of discovering what works best in the classroom. We used traditional materials in three consecutive classes (short documentaries as listening tasks followed by questions, vocabulary work, discussion, and role-play). Three weeks later, we used cartoons instead of documentaries, followed by the same type of activities. Upon reviewing these activities, we noticed that using cartoons helped stimulate and facilitate the learning of EFL. Our observations revealed that the students' attitudes were strikingly different when they were viewing the cartoons. They seemed to enjoy those classes more and participated more in the activities. We believe that cartoons motivated them and enhanced their desire to speak, as they wanted to comment on aspects of the cartoons.

Classroom implications

As oral communication seems to be a serious issue for DHH students, we relied on the idea advanced by Katchen (1995) that even the most unwilling student can be stimulated by the use of cartoons in class. So, the first activity we carried out in a mixed class of 16 students (three of whom were DHH)) was a comparison of *Little Red Riding Hood* by Walt Disney and *Red-Hot Riding Hood* by Tex Avery. The Walt Disney version is in the style of the classic fairy tale whereas, Tex Avery's version is a more contemporary adaptation. The students watched both versions several times and were asked to select any aspect of the cartoon and compare it across the two versions. This may have been a description of the characters, settings, clothes, plot, moral message, etc. Comprehension questions helped students to discuss the plot and learn new vocabulary and idiomatic expressions. The students then moved on to pair or group work to design their own version of the story, either in the form of a role play or the preparation of a new script of the fairy tale to be read aloud in class. This activity resulted in a more active, dynamic, and motivated class with relaxed students who were having fun while learning. For both options, the outcome was enjoyment for the students as well as the teacher. Although this class activity is nothing new as a pedagogical action, we noticed a change in the students' attitudes. We consider this viewing activity as fruitful because the students were willing to speak and communicate with each other, whatever the difficulty they encountered or effort they had to make. They were happy to communicate in sign and gesture too. We also noticed that they were eager to attend the following class at which there were follow-up activities. The results of this action research allowed us to observe the fact that the use of cartoons had changed the class atmosphere and "Shortly, the role of the learner is not to be a passive viewer but an active member in the triangle of the video, the teacher and the learner" (Çakir, 2006).

Building skills

When cartoons are implemented to teach DHH learners in the EFL classroom, the learners' attention is focused on the listening comprehension, while the visual aspects help them to understand and learn other details about the cartoon, smoothing the input and progress of oral communication. Çakir (2006, p. 68) describes this effectiveness of visual clues in boosting and facilitating the learning of the target language:

> The learner can also concentrate in detail on visual clues to meaning such as facial expression, dress, gesture, posture and on details of the environment. Even without hearing the language spoken, clues to meaning can be picked up from the vision alone. Using visual clues to meaning in order to enhance learning is an important part of video methodology.

It is apparent that cartoons provide DHH students with an appropriate medium to learn effectively. When DHH learners are active in class, they are more likely to be receptive to multiple communication strategies. For instance, the combination of sound and vision with paralinguistic features (mentioned in the previous section) can be a help for students when producing their own performances. In this context, the listening and understanding tasks are not only based on auditory input, so the students can still pick up the language. If our main target of this pedagogical activity is to help DHH students learn EFL in a relaxed and conducive environment, learning strategies come into play as a second and crucial target (O'Malley, 1990). The combination of sound, vision, and various paralinguistic features is beneficial to the students because it helps them to build a wide range of strategies. For example, active involvement in class facilitates the development of compensatory strategies like the ones cited by Oxford "(e.g. guessing from the context in listening, and strictly for speaking, using gestures or pause words) help learners to make up for missing knowledge" (Oxford, 2003, p. 13). DHH students need additional strategies to enhance their oral communication, for instance some social strategies, which facilitate communication achievements in class. Such strategies could include

> Asking questions to get verification, asking for clarification of a confusing point, asking for help in doing a language task, talking with a native-speaking conversation partner, and exploring cultural and social norms, help the learner work with others and understand the target culture as well as the language.
>
> (Oxford 2003, p. 14)

These strategies are closely linked to the intrinsic motivation mentioned in the first part of this paper, where doing an activity is for its inherent satisfaction. This is especially beneficial for hearing-impaired learners because these strategies can help them obtain and clarify missing information. The auditory activity in this context will not be the only means of conveying the message and giving access to cognitive interpretation and understanding. Cartoons, by their enjoyable nature, are a kind of gateway to communication and exchange.

The value of humour in the learning process is well known (Pollak, 1997). Humour, such as that seen in cartoons, can help establish an optimistic learning environment. Parrott (1994) suggests that cartoons have direct benefits: students have more creativity, more motivation, higher productivity, and more divergent thinking.

These results are mainly based on classroom observations, but our action research as EFL teachers suggests that using cartoons with DHH students is advantageous and does not only enhance oral communication but also supports the building of social learning strategies. It is well recognized that learning strategies are of the greatest relevance to EFL pedagogy (Oxford, 1990).

Conclusion

The aim of this pilot study through class observation research is to give an account of the benefits of using cartoons in the classroom and how they can enhance oral communication. The observation was focused on DHH students, particularly their degree of motivation and their involvement in the communicative tasks. Because of their multiple advantages, as shown in this chapter, the use of cartoons generated an enjoyable and relaxed atmosphere that prompted DHH students to take part in the oral activities, including paralinguistic elements to facilitate understanding and improve communication. The observation showed that cartoons may boost intrinsic motivation and enable a focus on new learning strategies, thus helping to enhance oral communication.

References

Bainbridge, C. (2015). Intrinsic motivation. Retrieved on 20th March 2018 from AboutParenting.com: http://giftedkids.about.com/od/glossary/g/intrinsic.htm

Bochner, J. H. (1982). English in the deaf population. In D. G. Sims, G. G. Walter, & R. L. Whitehead (Eds.), *Deafness and communication: Assessment and training* (pp. 107–123). Baltimore, MD: Williams and Wilkins.

Çakir, I. (2006). The use of video as an audio-visual material in foreign language teaching classroom. *The Turkish Online Journal of Educational Technology – TOJET, 5*(4), Article 9. ISSN: 1303–6521.

Clark, C. (2000). Innovative strategy: Concept cartoons. *Instructional and Learning Strategies, 12*, 34–45.

Doring, A. (2002). Effective teaching and learning at university: The use of cartoons as a teaching and learning strategy. *Australian Catholic University, 30*(1), 56–62.

Gilmore, A. (2007). Authentic materials and authenticity in foreign language learning. *Language Teaching, 40*, 97–118.

Hemei, J. (1997). Teaching with video in an English class. *Journal of English Teaching Forum, 35*(2), 45–47.

Katchen, J. E. (1993). Thanksgiving activities with *A Charlie Brown Thanksgiving*. *Video Rising, 5*(2), 7.

Katchen, J. E. (1995). How to use cartoons in the EFL classroom. *Thai TESOL Bulletin, 8*(1), 32–39.

Kemp, J. E. (1963). *Planning and producing audio-visual materials*. CA: Chandler Publishing Company.

Lewin, K. (1946). Action research and minority problems. *Journal of Social Issues, 2*(4), 34–46.

Lochrie, K. (1992). Using cartoons as an effective learning and teaching strategy. *SCRE Newsletter, 51*, 8–9.

Mains, E. (1945). The cartoon and the teaching of grammar. *The English Journal, 34*(9), 506–507.

Mustika, R. P. (2010). Improving Pronunciation Ability Using Cartoon Films (A Collaborative Action Research of the Eighth Grade Students of SMPN 1 Kaliwiro in 2009/2010). Retrieved on 4 April 2018 from: https://www03.core.ac.uk/download/pdf/12346825.pdf

Nunan, D. (1999). *Second language teaching and learning*. Boston: Heinle and Heinle Publishers.

O'Malley, J. M., & Chamot, A. U. (1990). *Learning strategies in second language acquisition*. Cambridge: Cambridge University Press

Oxford, R. L. (1990). *Language learning strategies: What every teacher should know*. Boston: Heinle & Heinle

Oxford, R. L. (2003). Language learning styles and strategies: An overview. *Learning Styles & Strategies, GALA*. Retrieved 25 April 2017 from http://web.ntpu.edu.tw/~language/workshop/read2.pdf

Parasnis, I. (1997). Cultural identity and diversity in deaf education. *American Annals of the Deaf, 142*(42), 72–79.

Parrott, T. (1994). Humour as a teaching strategy. *Nurse Educator, 19*(3), 36–38.

Pollak, J., & Freda, P. (1997). Humor, learning and socialization in middle level classrooms. *Clearing House, 70*(4), 176–178.

Rae, L. (2000). Effective Planning in Training and Development. Kogan Page. 1st edition.

Rule, A. C., & Auge, J. (2005). Using humorous cartoons to teach mineral and rock concepts in sixth grade science class. *Journal of Geoscience Education, 53*(3), 548–558.

Ryan, R. M., & Deci, E. L. (2000). Intrinsic and extrinsic motivations: Classic definitions and new directions. *Contemporary Educational Psychology, 25*, 54–67.

Wittich, W. A., & Schuller, C. F. (1953). *Audio-visual materials: Their nature and use*. Aurora, IL: Harper and Brothers Company.

4 Bringing film to English as a foreign language for the deaf and hard of hearing class

Anna Podlewska

Introduction

With the advent of digital technology and proliferation of mobile devices such as smartphones and tablets, which allow us to watch and record videos anywhere and at any time, moving images have come to play a key role in our everyday communication. At the same time, it has become much easier to integrate film into language courses, and English as a foreign language (EFL) courses for deaf and hard of hearing (DHH) students are no exception. Among the beneficial side effects of using film in language education and building a strong pedagogy around video materials are greater inclusiveness, increased motivation and willingness to perform in- and out-of-class activities, exposure to authentic language, and more opportunities to practise speech reading skills in the target language. Inclusiveness is particularly important for DHH learners. As Kieran Donaghy (2015, p. 16) put it in his book *Film in Action*:

> While film use is an effective educational tool for all learners, its positive effect on special populations of learners is gaining greater attention. There is an increasing body of empirical research that shows that moving image texts are very effective at reaching and empowering children with learning disabilities or economic disadvantages. . . . The ability of film to inspire increases even more when learners are actively involved in making their own moving image texts. Learners are usually highly enthusiastic, and prepared to put in a huge amount of time and effort when working on a moving image project because it is their own and it has a tangible result. Even learners who are normally disaffected and disengaged are happy to work on moving image projects in their own time, and often achieve excellent results.

Film is thus an inclusive medium, which by virtue of its visual and auditory content, contributes to learner engagement. Furthermore, unlike the vast majority of course books for EFL learners, online video materials can bridge the gap between the classroom and real life by providing learners with opportunities to discuss topics that really matter to them on a personal, moral, or global level. Prompts for discussion and writing may be found in video clips, short films, and feature-length films that deal with such contemporary issues as human rights, racism, consumerism, special educational needs, and genetic engineering, and which feature people with disabilities as protagonists. They may also be used as a starting point for reflecting on personal experiences and values like kindness, justice, and empathy.

When using videos in the classroom, the choice of material and accompanying activities must be carefully considered and adapted to the needs of each group or individual student in the case of one-to-one sessions.[1] If class participants want to work on their listening and if they use speech and hearing as their main form of communication, the classroom should provide good acoustics. Care should be taken to reduce the main factors that negatively affect this. Background noise[2] and reverberation[3] should be reduced by softening any hard surfaces. The classroom should be fitted with carpets, sound insulation, cork wallpaper, and blinds. Gaps between the walls and floor ought to be closed with sealant.[4] It is also helpful to position students near the teacher or other sound sources. Furthermore, in order for a student to make the most of their residual hearing, it is essential that their hearing aids, cochlear implants, and/or assistive listening devices are working properly, and that the equipment is carefully monitored.

Video captioning, either prepared in advance for pre-recorded material or typed live, is a powerful tool that should be used in EFL classes to facilitate comprehension and improve fluency. Captioning also enables DHH students to pick out any language that they consider particularly useful, apt, difficult, or confusing. Moreover, isolated onscreen texts, captions, or video scripts can be used by the teacher to create additional gap-fill, word choice, and pronunciation activities. If captions are not already available on the video, they can be created with the help of online caption editors such as Amara.org, Captiontube.appspot.com, Overstream.net, or free software such as Subtitle Edit. In addition, the most popular video hosting site, YouTube, has a feature that not only allows one to caption videos but also includes a tool for transcribing spoken language.[5] Yet, despite all the aforementioned advantages of captioning, it is important to note that those DHH students who have not yet developed age-appropriate language skills in their national and foreign languages will not be able to fully benefit from onscreen text. As Derek Brinkley (2011, p. 88) states:

> It makes no difference what is typed on screen if they [DHH students with limited language] cannot understand it, or if it has flashed on to the next sentence before they have worked out what it said, or if they are having to concentrate so hard on reading the subtitles that they do not have time to watch what is happening on the film.

To put it another way, in order to maximize learning outcomes when showing videos in class, teachers who have a comprehensive grasp of their DHH students' learning needs should be prepared to look out for these problems and provide additional explanations and background information where necessary.

Pre-existing video content in EFL for the DHH class

The following seven overviews are intended as detailed suggestions of videos that can be used in class, along with tried and tested tasks designed around them. They constitute practical examples of some possible uses of video resources. The activities presented here are generic and can be adapted to various types of films. The selected video material is suitable for older teens and young adults.

Overview 1

Signs (2008) is a 12-minute film directed by Patrick Hughes. It tells the story of Jason and Stacey, two young professionals who work in opposite office blocks. The couple communicate with each other using subtitle-like messages written on sheets of paper. This coy courtship leads to their eventual meeting. In general, DHH teenagers and young adults find the video relevant, engaging, and appealing, especially the unique form of communication employed by the protagonists. This short film can be used as support for teaching *going to* and *will/won't* + infinitive to make predictions.

> Language level: pre-intermediate (A2) – intermediate (B1)
> Topic: relationships/communication
> Language focus: *going to* and *will/won't* + infinitive used to make predictions
> Time: 60 minutes

Before you show the video

You might want to pre-teach and/or demonstrate the meaning of words and phrases such as:

> *to ask someone out on a date, a burglary, to keep on doing something, to reprimand, to pull the blinds down, to catch sunbeams in a mirror*

Procedure

1   Tell your students that they are going to watch a short film entitled *Signs*. Explain that you will be pausing the video as they watch, and that their task will be to predict what happens next. Each time, they will be given two options to choose from.

2   Give each student a copy of the worksheet and ask them to cover it with either a sheet of paper or a notebook.
3   Show the film and pause it at 01:19.
4   Ask individual students: What's going to happen next? What will happen next? Tell them to uncover the first two alternatives and to pick the one they think is more probable.
5   Play the next part of the video so that they can check whether they were right. If they picked the right option, they score a point. Repeat the procedure until you have shown the whole video. The pause times are indicated on the right side of the worksheet. The student with the highest score is the winner.

Answers

1 – B
2 – A
3 – B
4 – A
5 – A
6 – A
7 – B
8 – B

1   (01:19)

A) Jason is going to ask the girl out on a date.
B) Jason will smile at the girl, but he will not talk to her.

2   (03:09)

A) Jason will notice a girl.
B) Jason will notice a burglary.

3   (03:51)

A) The girl will keep on working.
B) The girl will write Jason a message on a sheet of paper.

4   (04:34)

A) The girl's next message will be: *Nice to meet you.*
B) The girl's next message will be: *What's your telephone number?*

5   (05:16)

A) Jason is going to fall off his chair.
B) Jason is going to be reprimanded by his boss in front of his colleagues.

6   (07:02)

A) Jason's next message will be: *Do you want to meet?*
B) Jason's next message will be: *I don't believe you!*

7   (08:26)

A) Stacey will be flirting with another man.
B) Stacey will not be in her office.

8   (09:47)

A) Jason will pull the blinds down.
B) Jason will look up and see Stacey catching sunbeams in a mirror.

After you watch

You may like to ask your students one last time: What's going to happen next? You might also want to discuss different methods of voiceless communication with your students.

Optional extension: the oracle

Ask the students what people do when they want to find out what future awaits them. Possible answers include the following: see a fortune-teller, read horoscopes, read tea leaves. Ask them what the ancient Greeks and Romans used to do to predict the future. If your students do not know, explain that they went to see the oracle. Then tell the students that in a moment, they are going to consult the oracle. Put the students into teams of two or three and give each team a copy of the worksheet and one die. Go through the instructions and demonstrate how to tackle the activity. Explain the meaning of any vocabulary items or phrases that your students do not understand. Then ask them whether they would like the oracle's predictions to come true.

*   Choose a question you want to ask.
*   Take turns rolling the die with the question in your mind.
*   Find a letter corresponding to your question (left-hand outer column of the grid) and the number you threw on the die (top row of the grid). Find your answer where the letter and the number meet.

Questions

*   What will the love of my life look/be like?
*   Will I be famous one day?
*   Will I travel the world?
*   How many children will I have?

	1.	2.	3.	4.	5.	6.
A)	Not as you expect. You'll be tempted by a bloke/chick with a hip-hop music collection.	Gorgeous! You'll attract a guy/girl with Celtic roots.	Not classically good-looking, but you'll never look at anybody else.	Very fit. He/she will be more outgoing than you are. You'll meet each other via a social networking site.	He/she will have wonderful eyes and very strong political views.	He/she'll look like you.
B)	No, you won't.	No, but you'll meet someone famous.	You'll be well-known in your profession.	You'll be in the news for doing something crazy.	You'll have your 15 minutes of fame.	Yes, but you'll have to work very hard.
C)	Yes, for pleasure.	Yes, for your job.	No, but you'll travel in your own country.	No, but you'll meet people from all over the world.	You'll have wonderful holidays abroad.	You'll travel when you're older.
D)	More than you expect.	The same number as your parents.	Your career will be more important.	One boy and one girl.	You'll have a big family.	Enough.
E)	At home, in bed.	In the mountains.	Abroad.	Near the sea.	Everywhere.	In a big city.
F)	Completely different.	Like your mother.	Younger than you are.	No different.	Like your father.	Absolutely fabulous!

- Where will I be the happiest?
- What will I look like in ten years' time?

Notes and comments

The extension task is a slightly altered version of the activity presented in the *Inside Out Student's Book Pre-intermediate* (Kay, Jones, & Kerr, 2002).

Overview 2

Word as Image (2011) is a short film created to promote a book by Ji Lee, a designer and creative director at Facebook. The film showcases a clever set of calligrams that depict the meanings of various words. These visualizations may be used to facilitate vocabulary learning and recall.

> Language level: pre-intermediate (A2) – intermediate (B1)
> Topic: word images
> Language focus: vocabulary; past simple and past continuous used for short, completed actions and actions in progress respectively
> Time: 60 minutes
> Introduce the topic by showing your students a still frame of the clock word image from the *Word as Image* video.
> Ask your students to come up with some more examples of word images in either English or their native languages.

Procedure

1   Explain that the students are going to watch a short video that presents animated word images similar to the one you have just shown.
2   Play the video.
3   Give the students two minutes to write down the words that they can remember on a piece of paper.
4   Ask your students how many words they have managed to memorize and why they remembered those specific words. You may want to tell them that forming mental images of vocabulary items is a useful mnemonic device.[6]
5   Play the video again and ask your students to write down all the words. As you watch, make sure they understand the meaning of every vocabulary item on the screen. Translate the new words into your students' national spoken and signed languages if necessary and provide example sentences.

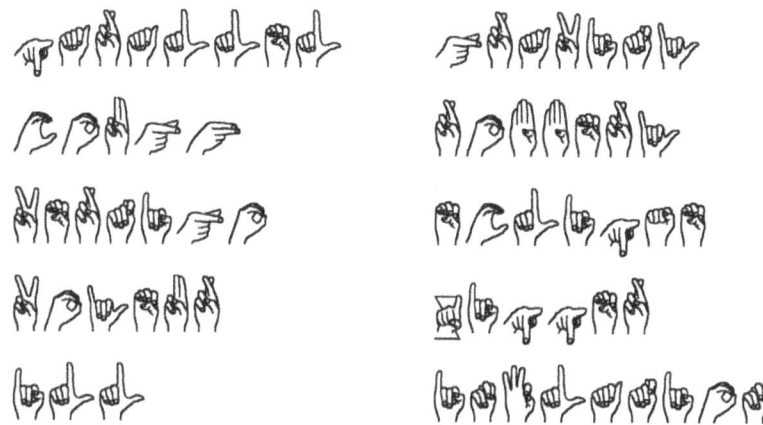

Figure 4.1 Fingerspellings of ten vocabulary items from the *Word as Image* video

The words include *idea, horizon, elevator, gravity, comedy, drama, capitalism, oil, the last supper, vampire, robbery, inflation, stock market, vertigo, voyeur, silicone, ill, balloons, tsunami, Spiderman, zipper, clock, pirate, exit, magic, fast food, diet, moon, parallel, tunnel, Marilyn, rabbit, homosexuals, heterosexuals, condom, cough, superstitious, Dali, Van Gogh,* and *eclipse.*

After you have watched

Ask your students to use an ASL manual alphabet diagram to match the listed vocabulary items from the *Word as Image* video with their corresponding fingerspellings (Figure 4.1). An example diagram can be found at https://dssofgcsc.wordpress.com/for-professors/types-of-sign-language/.

Answers

PARALLEL
COUGH
VERTIGO
VOYEUR
ILL
GRAVITY
ROBBERY

ECLIPSE
ZIPPER
INFLATION

Optional extension

1   Conduct a fingerspelling bee. Divide the class into small teams of two
    to three students and ask them to take turns fingerspelling the vocabu-
    lary items from the *Word as Image* video. The students who are not
    fingerspelling should write the word that is being fingerspelled by
    their team member. Students score one point for each correctly writ-
    ten vocabulary item. The student with the most points at the end of the
    game is the winner. If you teach on a one-to-one basis, you can com-
    pete with your student.
2   Explain that the students are going to take turns telling a story which
    begins as follows:

> *Last summer, I was staying with my friend Marilyn in Spain. The
> weather was sunny and we were sunbathing on the beach. Suddenly
> my phone rang. It was . . .*

The aim is to subtly include one word from the video in every fragment of the story. While the students are telling the story, note down
any errors that can be used for the correction activity described in the
following section.

Follow up

1   Prepare a *Mistakes bet, Grammar auction,* or *Spot the mistake* activity
    using the errors you noted down while your students were telling the
    story.
2   For homework, ask the students to write down the story they told in
    class.
3   You might also want to use a downloadable exercise devised by Kieran
    Donaghy. Link: http://film-english.com/2011/11/11/word-as-image/

The videos in Overviews 3 and 4 that follow are both entries uploaded onto
YouTube by popular vloggers. Vloggers typically upload their own films
for which they own the copyright and are happy for their work to be viewed
by as many people as possible so that they can accumulate high numbers of
views and subscribers. Therefore, teachers do not have to obtain permission
to show these sorts of YouTube videos in class.

Overview 3

Prom Dress Shopping Fail + Would You Rather! is a Kavari sisters' vlog entry in which the sisters go shopping together with their two male friends. On their way to various shops, they play 'Would You Rather'.

Language level: intermediate (B1) – advanced (C1)
Topic: free time activities
Language focus: vocabulary related to leisure activities; *would rather* followed by the infinitive without *to*, used to mean 'would prefer to'
Time: 60 minutes

Before you show the video

Introduce the topic by asking the students whether they watch any vlogs. Encourage them to give you examples of different types of vlogs. You might want to pre-teach the following vocabulary items: *prom, immortal, bare, significant other, nostril,* and *hobo.*

Procedure

1   Tell the students that they are going to watch a vlog entry in which a group of friends (Nazanin, Yasmin, Luis, and Rocky) are shopping for prom dresses and hanging out. Play part 1 (00:00–1:40) and ask the students to answer the following questions:

a)   How many people are wearing sunglasses?
b)   Where do they stop on the way to the dress store?
c)   Where is Rocky from?
d)   What picture did the driver post on the Internet?

Answers

a)   Three out of four people are wearing sunglasses.
b)   They stop at Starbucks.
c)   Rocky is from Shanghai, China.
d)   The driver posted a picture of his muscular legs.

2   Explain that the next segment shows the friends playing a game of, 'Would You Rather'. Ask the students to write down the questions that the friends ask each other. Explain that the students should try to understand as much as possible from what is being said. Then play part

2 (1:41–4:55) the whole way through. Play part 2 again if necessary, pausing after each question. If your students struggle with lip-reading in English, the alternative way of conducting this exercise is to give them the questions and ask them to put the questions in the order they are asked in the video.

'Would You Rather' questions; set 1

a) _____ Would you rather know the date of your death or the cause of your death?

b) _____ Would you rather use your bare hands to end the life of a human baby or a hundred cute puppies?

c) _____ Would you rather sit in a bucket full of worms for 30 minutes or eat five spiders/one spider?

d) _____ Would you rather be able to talk to animals or be able to speak all foreign languages?

e) _____ Would you rather be half your height or double your weight?

f) _____ Would you rather be the richest person on the planet or be immortal?

g) _____ Would you rather find true love or ten million dollars?

h) _____ Would you rather be caught cheating or catch your significant other cheating?

i) _____ Would you rather have the ability to give yourself more time or more money?

Answers

I Would you rather sit in a bucket full of worms for 30 minutes or eat five spiders/one spider?

II Would you rather find true love or ten million dollars?

III Would you rather know the date of your death or the cause of your death?

IV Would you rather have the ability to give yourself more time or more money?

V Would you rather be the richest person on the planet or be immortal?

VI Would you rather be half your height or double your weight?

VII Would you rather use your bare hands to end the life of a human baby or a hundred cute puppies?

VIII Would you rather be caught cheating or catch your significant other cheating?

IX Would you rather be able to talk to animals or be able to speak all foreign languages?

3   Ask the students to watch part 3 of the vlog (4:56–11:00) and write
     at least four questions about it. You might want to pre-teach YOLO
     (an acronym for *you only live once*, similar in meaning to Latin *carpe
     diem*). Ask the students to work in pairs and ask each other the ques-
     tions that they have just written down.
4   Explain that the next segment shows the friends playing 'Would You
     Rather' again. Ask the students to write down the questions that the friends
     ask each other. Explain that the students should try to understand as much
     as possible from what is being said. Then play part 4 (11:01–12:23) the
     whole way through. Play part 4 again if necessary, pausing after each
     question. If your students struggle with lip-reading in English, the alterna-
     tive way of conducting this exercise is to give them the questions and ask
     them to put the questions in the order they are asked in the video.

'Would You Rather' questions; set 2:

a)   _____ Would you rather run your tongue down a New York City side-
     walk or press your tongue into a stranger's nostril?
b)   _____ Would you rather eat a bowl of vomit or lick a hobo's foot?
c)   _____ Would you rather be forced to wear wet socks for the rest of your
     life or only be allowed to wash your hair once a year?
d)   _____ Would you rather have a finger as a tongue or have tongues as
     fingers?
e)   _____ Would you rather receive a lifetime supply of meals from your
     favorite restaurant or a lifetime supply of free gasoline?

Answers

 I   Would you rather be forced to wear wet socks for the rest of your life
      or only be allowed to wash your hair once a year?
 II   Would you rather have a finger as a tongue or have tongues as fingers?
 III Would you rather run your tongue down a New York City sidewalk or
      press your tongue into a stranger's nostril?
 IV   Would you rather receive a lifetime supply of meals from your favorite
      restaurant or a lifetime supply of free gasoline?
 V   Would you rather eat a bowl of vomit or lick a hobo's foot?

5   Before you play part 5 (12:24–14:12), ask the students to predict what
     is going to happen next. You might want to ask them the following
     predictive questions:

     •   Where do you think they will go next?
     •   Will they play 'Would You Rather' again?

- How will this vlog entry end?
- Play part 5 so that your students can check their predictions.

6   If there is time, let your students watch the complete vlog entry at the end so they can enjoy it in full.

After you have watched

Ask the students to read the following sentences and complete them with one of the vocabulary items you discussed earlier.

1   The _____ they saw in the street had only one shoe and was wearing a torn pair of pants.
2   I hope to get old with my _____ by my side.
3   The smell of dinner filled their _____.
4   Catholics believe that the soul is _____.
5   A _____ is a formal dance party for high school students, held at the end of a school year.
6   She had killed a man with her _____ hands.

Answers

1   hobo
2   significant other
3   nostrils
4   immortal
5   prom
6   bare

Optional extension

Ask the students to imagine they are going to make a vlog entry about their day. Ask them to think of five moments in their day they would like to record. When the students are ready, ask them to work in pairs to share their ideas for the vlog. The students could record their vlog entries as homework. These could be watched in a later class.

Overview 4

The Friendzone Test is Kristopher London's vlog entry in which he takes a 'friendzone test' together with his friend and fellow YouTuber Nazanin Kavari.

Language level: intermediate (B1) – upper intermediate (B2)
Topic: favorite things
Language focus: questions
Time: 60 minutes

Before you show the video

Introduce the topic by asking the students whether they know what a 'friendzone test' is and whether they have ever taken one. Divide the class into pairs (with one student in each pair as 'A' and the other as 'B') and explain that they are going to take the Friendzone Test in order to find out how well they know their classmate. Display the list of questions below and read them one at a time. All As should write down their answer to the question. At the same time, all Bs should write down what they think their partner will write. Tell the students that anyone caught cheating will lose a point – this includes winking, nudging, and secret signals. Once everyone has written an answer, each pair can take turns reading their answers, with B reading out their answer first. Then all the Bs may write their answer to the next question and the As write down what they think their partner will write. Then each pair can again take turns reading their answers, with A going first. Scores should be noted by each player on their answer sheet. Each pair gets one point for every time they have matching answers. The game ends after all the questions have been read out, and the pair with the most points wins. You might want to pre-teach the phrase *pet peeve* (something that you dislike because it annoys you).

How well do you know your classmate – the Friendzone Test

1   What is your favorite color?
2   Have you ever answered or placed a personal ad?
3   Are you registered as an organ donor?
4   What is your favorite drink?
5   Who is your favorite YouTuber?
6   What is your biggest fear?
7   How much are you in debt right now?
8   What is your favorite sport?
9   If you could have one wish granted, what would it be?
10   What was the last item you bought online?
11   What is your favorite food?
12   What is your favorite social media platform?
13   What is your biggest pet peeve?

68   *Anna Podlewska*

14   Your classmate has bad breath. Do you a) tell them b) make jokes c) leave some mints on their desk?
15   If you could be with a celebrity, who would that be?
16   What is your favorite season?
17   What is your favorite cartoon?
18   What are you bad at?
19   Of these, what's your most attractive body part? a) face b) chest and arms c) legs and buttocks
20   If your house caught fire, what one possession would you try to save?

Procedure

1   Explain that the students are going to watch a vlog entry in which two friends, Kristopher and Nazanin, are taking the Friendzone Test. Give a copy of the questions to each student and ask them to tick the questions that Kristopher and Nazanin answer in the video. Play the whole video. Link: https://youtu.be/oLsVmM5RNq4.

Answers

Questions 1, 4, 5, 6, 8, 11, 12, 13, 15, 16, 17, and 18 should be ticked.

2   Play the video again and ask the students to try to note down Kristopher's and Nazanin's answers to the Friendzone Test questions.

Optional extension

Ask your students to record a vlog entry in which they take the Friendzone Test.
     The language teaching profession has been making use of film clips and feature-length films for decades. The main benefit of using the former is that it is fairly easy to find excerpts from TV series or feature films which aptly illustrate grammatical points or vocabulary and can serve as input for subsequent tasks. Since feature-length films are too long to watch in class, it is worth asking the students to watch them at home and to tackle the after-you-have-watched activities in class. The activities that accompany the videos in Overviews 5 and 6 involve exploiting an individual film clip for language study and pronunciation practice as well as responding to a complete film.

Overview 5

Friends is one of the most popular television sitcoms of all times. It revolves around a group of people living in Manhattan. *The One Where Ross Hugs Rachel* is the second episode of season six of the series.

Language level: pre-intermediate (A2) – intermediate (B1)
Topic: plans for the future
Language focus: *will* and *won't* used to express hopes about the future
Time: 60 minutes

Before you show the video

1   Introduce the topic by asking the students whether they like watching sitcoms like *Friends*. Encourage the students to tell you anything they know about the sitcom.
2   Tell the students that they are going to watch a short part of episode two from season six. You might want to pre-teach the following vocabulary items: *custody, filthy rich, to ditch,* and *to hook up*. Ask your students to match these words with their definitions.

   a)   very wealthy; usually used to say you think someone has too much money – _____
   b)   the right to take care of a child, given to one of their parents –
      _____
   c)   to start having a sexual relationship with someone –
      _____
   d)   to end a romantic relationship with someone –
      _____

Answers

a)   filthy rich
b)   custody
c)   to hook up
d)   to ditch

Procedure

1   Play the video (20:50–21:50) and ask the students to put the utterances in the order they hear them.

JOEY: So, Ross and Rachel got married. Monica and Chandler almost got married. You think you and I should hook up?
PHOEBE: Oh, we do, but not just yet.
_____ P: I know. Then, I'm **gonna** marry Chandler for the money and you'll marry Rachel and have the beautiful kids.

_____ P: I don't **wanna** go into the whole thing, but, um, we have words and I kill him.

_____ P: Um, ok, first Chandler and Monica will get married and be filthy rich, by the way, but, um, it won't work out.

_____ J: What about Ross?

_____ P: But then we ditch those two, and that's when we'll get married. We'll have Chandler's money and Rachel's kids. And getting custody will be easy because of Rachel's drinking problem.

_____ J: Really? When?

_____ J: Wow!

_____ J: Great!

Answers

JOEY: So, Ross and Rachel got married. Monica and Chandler almost got married. You think you and I should hook up?

PHOEBE: Oh, we do, but not just yet.

J: Really? When?

P: Um, ok, first Chandler and Monica will get married and be filthy rich, by the way, but, um, it won't work out.

J: Wow!

P: I know. Then, I'm **gonna** marry Chandler for the money and you'll marry Rachel and have the beautiful kids.

J: Great!

P: But then we ditch those two, and that's when we'll get married. We'll have Chandler's money and Rachel's kids. And getting custody will be easy because of Rachel's drinking problem.

J: Oh! What about Ross?

P: I don't **wanna** go into the whole thing, but, um, we have words and I kill him.

2   Ask the students whether they know what the words in bold mean. Explain that these forms are frequently used in speech in informal, colloquial English instead of *want to* and *going to*.

3   Tell the students that they are now going to dub the video. Explain that dubbing, also known as re-recording or voice acting, is a process of replacing actors' voices in a film or video with the voices of dubbers recorded later. Divide the class into pairs, A – Phoebe and B – Joey, and tell them to practise reading the transcript. Tell them to change roles once or twice.

4   Play the video with the sound and subtitles on and ask the students to dub the actors. Repeat the procedure until your students become confident with their performance.

5 Use the mute control to view the sequence without sound. Ask your students to reconstruct the conversation. Repeat the procedure several times until your students become confident with their performance.

6 Finally, you might want to record your students and put their voices in the sequence.

After you have watched

Divide the class into two groups, A and B. Tell your students to think about their future. Tell them to think of answers to the following questions:

Will you be richer than you are at the moment?
Will you live here or in another country?
Will you be married, single, or divorced?
Will you have children/more children/grandchildren?
Will you be fitter than you are at the moment?
Where will you be the happiest?
Will you be famous?
Will you speak English fluently?
Where will you travel?

Ask each student from group A to sit opposite one of the students from group B. Give the As three minutes to tell the Bs about their future. The Bs' task is to write down any mistakes they think the As might have made and to give feedback. The students can change partners twice to become more fluent and confident. Then they can change roles and repeat the procedure so that now the Bs can tell the As about their future. Circulate, and monitor the class, paying attention to the correct use of future forms and noting down errors for correction. Then give your feedback to the whole class.

Notes and comments

The dubbing activity is based on an idea by Tomás Costal from Universidad Nacional de Educación a Distancia, Spain, who designed, developed, and implemented a didactic innovation initiative known as the English Project. For more information on this and its resources, see two public YouTube channels: Xunco English (link: https://goo.gl/ZP5kjM) and Xunco Students (link: https://goo.gl/vAoMcb).

Overview 6

Children of a Lesser God is the 1986 feature-length film version of Mark Medoff's play, which portrays the conflict between the deaf and hearing worlds. The film tells the story of John Leeds, an idealistic teacher, and Sarah Norman, a strong-willed deaf girl.

> Language level: intermediate (B1) and above
> Topic: perspectives of deafness; teacher-student relationships; romantic relationships
> Language focus: no specific focus
> Time: variable

Procedure

1   Explain that the students are going to view the film *Children of a Lesser God* at home, which will enable them to pause it and re-watch any scenes they do not understand.
2   After viewing the film, the students should write a 250-word reaction paper. Ask them to document their feelings, thoughts, and insights about the film. You might want to give them the following questions to consider:

> What did you like best about the film? Why?
> Was there anything you did not like about the film? Why?
> What are the perspectives of deafness presented in the film?
> How do those perspectives cause conflict?

3   Conduct a whole-class discussion based on the questions.

Similar to film clips and vlogs, trailers are widely available, conveniently short, and immediately engaging. However, since many of them are fast-paced, they may be difficult to follow and their linguistic content may be less contextualized. The challenge for the teachers is thus to exercise professional judgement to ensure that trailers shown in class benefit students' learning and do not cause frustration. The following activities designed around the trailer for *Frozen* encourage students to carefully observe and describe what happens in the video and give reactions to it.

Overview 7

Frozen is a Disney animated feature film that tells the story of a princess who sets out on a journey to find her estranged sister. The princess is accompanied by an iceman, his pet reindeer, and a snowman.

> Language level: intermediate (B1) and above
> Topic: putting a visual narrative into words

Language focus: verbs used to describe actions and movement
Time: 40 minutes

Before you show the video

Explain to the students that you are going to give them a worksheet of jumbled sentences that describe the things that happen in a film trailer with audio description for *Frozen*, a Disney animated feature film. Give each student a copy of the worksheet. Ask them to read the sentences to prepare themselves for putting them in chronological order. Go through the events line by line, eliciting and explaining any new vocabulary.

Procedure

1   Play the trailer (link: https://youtu.be/O7j4_aP8dWA) and ask the students to put the events in the order they see them happen.

_____ His nose lands on a frozen pond.

_____ Seeing the reindeer slip on the ice, the snowman smiles and moves towards him, though actually he's running in place.

_____ The snowman puts himself back together again and glumly contemplates his nose-less state.

_____ The reindeer jams the carrot back in place.

_____ The reindeer paddles his front legs.

_____ A carrot-nosed, coal-eyed snowman shuffles up to a purple flower peeping up out of the deep snow.

_____ He takes a deep sniff.

_____ A reindeer looks up and pants like a dog.

_____ The snowman uses his arm as a crutch.

_____ The reindeer does the breaststroke.

_____ The reindeer's tongue sticks to the ice.

_____ The twig arm and reindeer lips tug at the carrot.

_____ Head over heels, the snowman crawls over the ice.

_____ The snowman's head shoots off.

_____ The carrot flies off and lands in soft snow.

_____ The reindeer falls on his chin.

_____ The snowman rolls his body but flips onto his back.

_____ The reindeer goes after it with the snowman and his body parts hanging on his tail.

_____ The snowman pats him with a stick of an arm, then goes to sneeze.

_____ He grabs his nose with both hands.

Answers

A carrot-nosed, coal-eyed snowman shuffles up to a purple flower peeping up out of the deep snow.

> He takes a deep sniff.
> His nose lands on a frozen pond.
> A reindeer looks up and pants like a dog.
> Seeing the reindeer slip on the ice, the snowman smiles and moves towards him, though actually he's running on the spot.
> The reindeer falls on his chin.
> The snowman uses his arm as a crutch.
> The reindeer paddles his front legs.
> Head over heels, the snowman crawls over the ice.
> The reindeer does the breaststroke.
> The snowman rolls his body but flips onto his back.
> The reindeer's tongue sticks to the ice.
> The twig arm and reindeer lips tug at the carrot.
> The carrot flies off and lands in soft snow.
> The reindeer goes after it with the snowman and his body parts hanging on his tail.
> The snowman puts himself back together again and glumly contemplates his nose-less state.
> The reindeer jams the carrot back in place.
> The snowman pats him with a stick of an arm, then goes to sneeze.
> He grabs his nose with both hands.
> His head shoots off.

2   Ask the students to imagine that the film trailer is a live theatre event. Their task will be to provide an audio description service for this event. They can use the worksheet. Play the trailer without sound at least three times and have your students tackle the task together in unison. Then play the trailer several more times so that the students can practise individually.
3   During the following class, you might want to ask the students to perform the task again, but this time from memory.

After you have watched

Tell your students to imagine that one of their Facebook friends or a fellow YouTuber has just shared this trailer, and some people have already commented on it. Distribute an A4 sheet of paper with the following comments at the top:

JOE: I don't think I've ever been so appreciative of my sight as when trying to follow this with my eyes closed.

AJ: Honestly, "his head shoots off" added SO much humor to that scene. Like, it was a bit funny seeing it, but hearing it described so bluntly was 100x funnier.

MEL: Really good for language learning IMHO.

Ask the students to either write their own comments or react to these comments.

Notes and comments

This activity is based on an idea by Robert Campbell. Paper Facebook/ YouTube can also be used to introduce a particular topic.

Teacher-generated content in EFL for the DHH class

This chapter has presented several adaptable ideas on how to integrate short films, vlog entries, and excerpts from TV series, feature-length films, and trailers into a general EFL course for DHH learners. In other words, it has examined ways of exploiting pre-existing video content in class. We can now look at the practical applications of teacher-generated content.

Despite a clear improvement in the conditions for modern foreign language (FL) learning both in the state educational system and on the open market for educational services in Europe, it is still virtually impossible for DHH students to access such basic materials as the audio recordings that sometimes accompany course books. Apart from conversations, these recordings often contain street noise and music which make the listening extremely challenging. An example of an effective solution to this problem is for the teacher to create videos intended to offer a visual representation of the texts in the course book.[7] This can be done with a simple device such as a phone or tablet. The resulting videos can then be edited in Windows Movie Maker or other free-licensed software and shared with the students. This may also require the participation of at least one expert English speaker who is capable of sustaining clear articulation over extended periods of time and feels comfortable in front of a camera. Your speaker may want to either read or recite the listening text from memory. If your students are familiar with the American or British version of the cued speech system, you could consider fluent cuers in your search for expert speakers. Cuers are often capable of using their right and left hand alternately to convey the utterances of two interlocutors. It is not necessary for you and your speaker(s) to meet in person; videos can be created through chat applications such as Skype and screencast software. Alternatively, teachers may record themselves.

Teacher-generated content exploits a medium that is already familiar to learners. Such videos are designed to be watched on a portable device at the students' convenience, so they facilitate learning on the go and self-study outside the classroom. This means that they have the added advantage of promoting learner autonomy and helping DHH students take ownership of their language development.

Conclusion

The strategies recommended in this chapter for adapting listening texts to the needs and abilities of DHH students is based largely on suggestions obtained from the students themselves. Their practical utility has been checked in the classroom. Students who are regularly exposed to English via the audio-visual or audio-visual-manual modality report that they are able to tackle listening tasks that would be impossible in the auditory modality alone.

To summarize, due to its accessibility, engaging content, multimodality, interactivity, and inclusive nature, video material has continued to open up new possibilities for FL teachers and their students. The suggestions for video use presented in this chapter may be helpful for novice teachers, particularly in integrated settings. The advice given here on incorporating video activities into lesson plans will hopefully become a springboard for their own original teaching ideas. These ideas and their implementation and relationship to learning outcomes can then be explored in systematic research.

Notes

1 For more information on the adaptation of teaching materials in English language instruction for students with hearing impairments, see Podlewska (2012). For more information on strategies for teaching EFL to DHH learners, see Domagała-Zyśk and Karpińska-Szaj (2011).
2 Background or ambient noise – the amount of noise going on in the classroom before the conversation or listening takes place.
3 Reverberation – the time it takes for a sound to dissipate. It takes longer for this to happen when a sound bounces off hard surfaces. Short reverberation times can make the speech signal clearer. In general, rooms for the performance of non-amplified music require longer reverberation times than rooms for speech.
4 Further information on how to create an optimal listening environment can be found in Easterbrooks and Estes (2007).
5 See Sutherland (2008) for more discussion of the benefits of using captioned videos.
6 For more information about how our brains process visual information as opposed to text and sound, see the work of Allan Paivio (1986, 1991), a psychology professor from the University of Western Ontario, who was the first to introduce

the dual-coding theory. According to this theory, pictures are encoded both visually and verbally and are thus easier to recall. Polish speakers can get more information on mnemonic devices from an online presentation by Edyta Madej. Link: www.pearson.pl/angielski/konferencje-szkolenia/filmy-szkoleniowe-385/mnemotechniki-jako-wsparcie-w-nauce-jezykow-obcych-3422.html

7 For practical tips on framing, choosing locations, and using video chat applications, see Keddie (2014).

References

Brinkley, D. (2011). *Supporting deaf children and young people: Strategies for intervention, inclusion and improvement*. London: Continuum.

Clark, J. M., & Paivio, A. (1991). Dual coding theory and education. *Educational Psychology Review, 3*(3), 149–170.

Domagała-Zyśk, E., & Karpińska-Szaj, K. (2011). *Uczeń z wadą słuchu w szkole ogólnodostępnej*. Kraków: Oficyna Wydawnicza Impuls.

Donaghy, K. (2015). *Film in action*. Peaslake: Delta Publishing.

Easterbrooks, S., & Estes, E. (2007). *Helping deaf and hard of hearing students to use spoken language: A guide for educators and families*. Thousand Oaks, CA: Corwin Press, Sage.

Kay, S., Jones, V., & Kerr, P. (2002). *Inside out student's book: Pre-intermediate*. Oxford: Macmillan Publishers.

Keddie, J. (2014). *Bringing online video into the classroom*. Oxford: Oxford University Press.

Paivio, A. (1986). *Mental representations*. New York: Oxford University Press.

Podlewska, A. (2012). Adaptacja materiałów dydaktycznych w nauce języka angielskiego studentów z dysfunkcją słuchu. In Z. Palak, D. Chimicz, & A. Pawlak (Eds.), *Wielość obszarów we współczesnej pedagogice specjalnej* (pp. 383–390). Lublin: Wydawnictwo UMCS.

Sutherland, I. M. (2008). Everybody wins: Teaching deaf and hearing students together. In T. Berberi, E. C. Hamilton, & I. M. Sutherland (Eds.), *Worlds apart? Disability and foreign language learning* (p. 59). New Haven, CT: Yale University Press.

Part 2

Contexts and outcomes

5 Individual differences in deaf learners' second language acquisition

Jitka Sedláčková

Introduction

The foreign language teaching of deaf learners is still a relatively new field. Although activity in this field has been on the rise since the beginning of the century (see for example Mole, McColl, & Vale, 2005; Kellett Bidoli & Ochse, 2008; Csizér, Kontra, & Piniel, 2015; Domagała-Zyśk, 2015; Domagała-Zyśk & Kontra, 2016), there is still a scarcity of both published research results and methodological guides based on well-evidenced practice.

In connection with the current trend for inclusion and equal access to education, however, more and more teachers at all levels of education can encounter DHH students in their classes. The teaching of such students is specialized in many respects, particularly with regard to the means of communication, which is an especially tricky issue for foreign spoken language instruction. Language teachers, who often do not have a background in teaching students with special educational needs (SEN), are thus faced with an entirely new situation. Even for teachers who are trained in SEN or who have some degree of experience in teaching DHH students, there is a lack of research-based methodological guidelines and examples of good practice, which makes it difficult for them to develop their teaching beyond the method of trial and error and reduce the need to constantly create their own materials and teaching resources.

Apart from placing increased demands on the educators, the lack of resources in the field may also lead to an increased tendency to generalize the few research results or examples of good practice that are available (see Marschark et al., 2017). The present chapter highlights the importance of approaching each student individually and focuses on increasing teachers' awareness of the areas of possible differences among individual DHH learners.

The objective of the chapter is to stress the need for an individual approach to deaf learners in the foreign language classroom. To pursue this objective, the chapter draws upon the existing knowledge of individual differences in second language learning/acquisition (the abbreviation 'SLA' is used as an umbrella term for the two concepts throughout the chapter) among hearing learners, and develop it further in relation to deaf learners.

Although many specificities that affect foreign language learning concern almost all DHH persons regardless of the extent of hearing loss, including cochlear implant users (Marschark et al., 2012), they are most distinctly expressed in persons with a profound or total loss of hearing. This is also the group which is most covered by research. For these reasons, the present chapter focuses on profoundly prelingually D/deaf learners.

The practical examples of the possible differences among these learners in relation to SLA are based on research conducted by the author with D/deaf English as a foreign language (EFL) learners at the university level. The research was designed as a multiple case study and its qualitative character allowed for an interpretation that included the respondents' views of the issues. The methodology is described in previous publications (see Sedláčková, 2016).

Areas of difference

From the point of view of SLA, DHH learners in no respect form a homogeneous group. Firstly, we need to take into account the individual learning differences in SLA (see Oxford, 1990; Dörnyei & Skehan, 2003; Ellis, 2004; Dörnyei, 2005), which apply to DHH learners as well as to other learners. And secondly, the differences may be further conditioned or accentuated by the type and expression of an individual's hearing loss, previous language development, preferred means of communication, educational history, and so on.

The traditionally discussed individual differences in SLA include age, language aptitude, cognitive styles, learning strategies, and affective factors such as motivation, anxiety, and so on. The individual differences, needs, and preferences of a learner constitute a complex dynamic system of mutually interacting factors which impact the rate, route, and achievement of language learning (Ellis, 2004). These factors differ among individual learners, including DHH learners. The present chapter focuses mainly on age and affective factors and discusses the possible ways in which these can be influenced by deafness.

Hearing loss: different views and different impacts

The medical perspective on hearing loss seems to offer a fairly objective distinction. According to the classification of the World Health Organization

(2012), several groups can be distinguished based on the degree of hearing loss measured by an audiogram. A person can be hard of hearing (HOH) when the loss in decibels ranges from 25–70 dB, practically deaf with a loss of 70–90 dB, and profoundly deaf when the loss exceeds 90 dB. Secondly, hearing loss can be categorized according to the time of its development as either innate or acquired (Horáková, 2006). An important distinction here is between prelingually and postlingually deaf (deafened). Prelingual deafness constitutes profound loss of hearing at birth or before the basic development of speech, that is, before the age of 2 or 3.

The medically determined degree of hearing loss can be further modified by compensatory aids. For those with profound hearing loss, the most influential aid in question is likely to be a cochlear implant. Cochlear implantation and its impact on the D/deaf community is currently one of the topical issues in deaf studies. Irrespective of this debate, it needs to be said that cochlear implantation as such does not present an ultimate solution to the problems of language and literacy development (Marschark et al., 2015).

The heterogeneity of DHH people is, however, primarily based not so much on the type and severity of one's hearing but on one's means of communication and life experiences. A supportive family environment and an early intervention seem to substantially influence the skills and abilities that are especially important in language learning. The hearing loss itself, in terms of anatomic or physiological structures and functions, says very little about the particular individual's abilities and preferences. Marschark et al. (2015) warn against the generalizing term *deaf*, which causes misunderstanding and overgeneralization of research findings and consequently their incorrect application in practice.

Differences in means of communication and their uses

DHH persons make use of various means of communication; their preference is based on the character of their hearing loss and family history as well as their identity. Their choice of communication method also depends on the other participants in the particular interaction. One option is sign language, which is a natural (i.e. not consciously invented) language independent of the structure of local spoken languages, with its own independent vocabulary and grammatical structures (Sandler & Lillo-Martin, 2002).

Neurobiological research has suggested that despite its visual-gestural character, sign language is processed predominantly in the left brain hemisphere and its processing in the short-term and long-term memory resembles that of spoken languages (Emmorey, 2002). Research findings also indicate that deaf children who are exposed to sign language acquire it in ways similar to the acquisition of spoken languages, in terms of both key turning points and rate. This fact offers support to the idea that both of the modalities represent the same cognitive system and share universal features (Bochner & Albertini, 1996; Sandler & Lillo-Martin, 2002).

The two main features that distinguish sign languages from spoken languages are simultaneity (as opposed to linearity) and the use of the three-dimensional space, which facilitates, for example, a distinct way of expressing space-time relations and the relationship between individual agents in an utterance. The differences between signed and spoken languages may cause interference in deaf people's use of spoken languages.

Various other systems have been developed to support the communication of DHH people, particularly to facilitate the comprehensibility of spoken language through visual means. Examples of such systems include cued speech and Visual Phonics. These systems are used mostly in educational settings rather than in everyday communication. For everyday communication, especially in families with hearing parents and deaf children, home signs are naturally developed (Sandler & Lillo-Martin, 2002). Communication between deaf and hearing persons is also typically facilitated by the use of written language and by lip-reading.

Different educational experiences

Apart from their first language experiences based on their family environment, deaf people also differ in their educational histories. Learners may have been educated in special or mainstream schools. Some learners may have experienced the oral method, which prioritizes the mastering of a spoken language, both in its spoken and written forms. Others might have participated in a school environment that mainly supported communication in sign language. Still others may have been educated in the idea of total communication, a system in which all available and possible expressive and receptive means (including spoken language, visualization, sign language, fingerspelling, speech, reading and writing, gestures, and mime) are used to enable communication from the start (Krahulcová, 2003). Furthermore, there is the bilingual approach, which acknowledges the equal status of signed and spoken languages. It stresses the acquisition of a sign language as a natural and fully accessible language and subsequent socialization, followed by the learning of a spoken language, particularly in its written form.

All of the circumstances described previously influence the development of the first language (or languages) in a DHH individual, making the issue rather complicated. Although many D/deaf individuals consider sign language to be their first language and spoken language to be their second language, this cannot be generalized to all (Bochner & Albertini, 1996). From the theoretical point of view this depends on the definition of the first language. This issue is unfortunately beyond the scope of this chapter and requires simplification. Both the local sign language and the local spoken language are usually, even if to different extents, involved in the early language development of D/deaf individuals and may therefore be included in the theoretical concept of 'first language' (L1).

Significance of L1 development for subsequent language learning

Why should foreign language teachers concern themselves with the development of learners' L1 and their achievement in it? Various authors argue that L1 development is a crucial factor influencing further language learning because learners' initial experience in using their first language leads to a neural attunement to it, which affects their SLA (Ellis & Larsen-Freeman, 2006; Larsen-Freeman & Cameron, 2008). In DHH persons, the development of first language, however, often presents a quite complicated issue.

A natural language development can take place when a DHH child is born to D/deaf parents who are sign language users. Then the development follows a similar path to hearing children, both in rate and in sequence because the child has access to a suitable and rich linguistic environment with comprehensible input (Bochner & Albertini, 1996; Paul, 2009; Spencer & Marschark, 2010). However, this represents only about 5% to 10% of deaf children (Marschark et al., 2015). The overwhelming majority of DHH children experience a very distinct language development. Due to the sensory barrier, spoken language cannot be perceived naturally. Additionally, the presence of sign language is limited, and thus many children with profound hearing loss find themselves in the earliest stages of their lives in an environment which Macurová (1998) describes as a state of early "non-language". As Knoors (2015, p. 21) concludes:

> [D]elayed access to language, in spoken or in signed form, will lead to negative consequences (especially in the field of complex grammar) that cannot be overcome, no matter how long and intensely a child or adolescent is exposed to first language input later.

A language is a basic instrument for thought and for gaining understanding of the world and of oneself. Through a language, relationships between the individual elements of the outside world are understood, arranged, and generalized (Gadamer, 1966). Language competences are also important for socialization, including the acquisition of forms of behavior and knowledge, and the values and culture of one's society. The fact that the developing experiences of some DHH children are not linked with language represents a further limitation in both their language and literacy development (McAnally, Rose, & Quigley, 2007).

The restrictions imposed on communication do not only influence language development in early life. Spencer and Marschark (2010) illustrate the negative impact on the acquisition of vocabulary and syntax and explain that even in later stages of the development, linguistic input is considerably limited by the impossibility of DHH persons to overhear conversations and interactions in their surroundings.

Despite the sensory accessibility of sign language, its availability particularly in early childhood is limited and access to proficient adult signers is rare (Knoors, 2015). A further constraint is represented by the absence of metalinguistic knowledge about the language, which consequently restricts the development of the language itself and also the functioning of the language as a basis for learning additional languages. There is some evidence that deaf individuals who do not acquire sign language from their parents from birth but start learning it after entering school (around the age of 5), never achieve native-like competence (Newport, 1990; Sandler & Lillo-Martin, 2002).

From what has been said so far, it is clear that the aspects in which DHH foreign language learners differ not only from hearing learners but also from one another are indeed multifarious. In the following section, two areas of deaf learners' individual differences are discussed. These include the age factor and affective factors. A variety of aspects and experiences are illustrated using the examples of three deaf EFL learners.

Age factor

One of the oft-discussed factors related to foreign language learning is age. The idea of a critical (sensitive) period of language acquisition, which basically supposes that in a certain period of life an individual learns (acquires) a language more easily than later on, when reaching the same level of language competence is either more difficult or even impossible, has been extended to SLA (DeKeyser, 2000). Although the issue is far from resolved, it seems to be clear that a distinction needs to be made between language acquisition (in a natural environment) and language learning (in a formal environment) (Najvar & Hanušová, 2010). Moreover, the age factor needs to be considered in relation to other linguistic, cognitive, and social factors (Jia, 2008).

As explained previously, an individual's L1 plays a significant role in his or her learning of a foreign language. In the area of foreign language learning, it is therefore necessary to take the factor of age into account in relation not only to the foreign language but also to the learner's L1. This might hold true in particular in situations when the L1 proficiency is problematic (Sparks & Ganschow, 1993). In DHH learners, the influence of both the local spoken and sign languages needs to be considered, not least because the proficiency in both is limited for many deaf learners (Macurová & Hanáková, 2011).

As already indicated, learners who are prelingually profoundly deaf may differ substantially in aspects influencing SLA. In the following paragraphs, findings from the research described previously are used to illustrate the possible dissimilarities in relation to the age factor in L1 and foreign language learning. Out of the three participants in the study, one came from a D/deaf family (with D/deaf parents and siblings and sign language as the main means of communication) and two were from hearing families (with hearing parents and siblings). Coming from a D/deaf family, Ron's early language development followed a path similar to hearing children; his sign language proficiency may be expected to be high and the determination of his L1 seems quite clear. In this respect, he is a representative of the small group of DHH children with signing D/deaf parents. Nonetheless, this seemingly straightforward development becomes more complicated when it comes to written language. His first experience of reading and writing was not in sign language but in the local spoken language. The different modalities of these languages and the non-existence of a written form of sign language make it problematic to determine the first language of written literacy.

Although the other two participants were from hearing families, they differed in their early language development, current language preferences, and proficiency prior to learning a foreign language (EFL). In both cases, the L1 development corresponded to a common scenario for many DHH children, which includes delayed access to a fully sensorily accessible language (sign language), its unsystematic acquisition, and the lack of adult language models in the early development stages. Even if their parents made an attempt to learn sign language to some degree, they could not learn it fluently within the short time period necessary to aid their child's first language acquisition, and their communication comprised a mixture of spoken language, lip-reading, home signs, gesticulation, and sign language, with the local spoken language being predominant. The early language environment was influenced mainly by the parents and thus differed on the basis of their education, involvement, and decisions about language, including their willingness and motivation to learn sign language. It was also influenced by the abilities of the individual child (e.g. intelligence or character). In the described situation, the development of either the local spoken language or local signed language on a par with hearing children cannot be expected to occur before preschool education.

Owing to the varied influences, the participants' views and competencies related to their L1 differed. One of the participants considered the local spoken language as his first and preferred language in daily communication, whereas another participant placed the local sign language in this position. Interestingly, both assessed their sign language proficiency as very good but restricted in comparison with signers brought up by deaf parents.

The proficiency of all the participants in the local spoken language, although it was not specifically measured in the study, can be described based on self-reported information and observable aspects of language production. The participants could understand its everyday written form (and spoken form with the help of lip-reading). All of them reported problems with reading academic, specialized, and literary texts containing figurative language and implied meanings. As observable from e-mail communication and online chat, although their written texts are generally comprehensible, they all make mistakes in the choice of lexis, grammar (e.g. verb phrases), and syntax.

It seems clear that the age factor should be a central consideration for not only foreign language learning but also the L1 development of DHH learners. Their L1 preferences and knowledge might differ considerably and can be expected to affect their SLA.

Affective factors

Affective factors like motivation and anxiety also represent areas in which foreign language learners differ from each other and which can influence the learning process and results. It has been determined that a safe and supportive environment plays a positive role in cognitive performance and the process of learning (Rudy, 2008). Considering what has been said so far, it can be expected that language learning (particularly of spoken languages) is connected to negative feelings for many DHH people (Easterbrooks & Beal-Alvarez, 2013). Nevertheless, as the following findings illustrate, this assumption cannot be taken for granted and does not apply to all deaf learners. Different experiences and personalities have important effects.

Firstly, none of the research participants expressed negative attitudes towards any of the languages they were using (i.e. their local spoken language, local sign language, and English), and they used the languages effectively to achieve their communicative purposes in various situations. The findings correspond to those of Herzig (2009) and Marschark et al. (2015).

Each of the participants expressed a slightly different attitude towards spoken/written language and their learning. Ron described how he first learned the local spoken language (and its written form) from children's picture books, motivated by his own curiosity. A high level of inner motivation contributed to the development of his language and reading skills, as he frequently read texts on his personal interests. Some negative comments were related to formal instruction of the local spoken language at school, which Ron seemed to consider ineffective. Based on his answers to questions about both the local spoken language and EFL, it can be inferred that personal motivation has played a large part in Ron's language development, outweighing the value he places on the language and his previous experiences with learning.

On the other hand, the second respondent, Tim, described several concrete examples of positive experiences connected with learning the local spoken language both at home and at school (e.g. reading with his mum and supportive teachers who showed interest and patience and helped him to understand the meaning of texts). Nonetheless, he repeatedly expressed his low motivation to learn languages, which also showed in his activity or rather inactivity with regard to his EFL development. For example, although Tim understood the benefit of reading for language development, he did not read in any language outside of school requirements. He also skipped his EFL homework regularly and could not be described as an independent learner.

The third respondent, Ann, represented yet a different set of experiences and preferences. Even though she regarded formal instruction in the local spoken language neutrally or slightly negatively (e.g. being forced to read aloud and answer comprehension questions rather than being supported in the understanding of texts), this does not seem to have had a negative influence on her perception of formal language learning in general. On the contrary, thanks to a supportive EFL teacher, Ann became highly motivated and eventually decided to study English as her major at university.

These examples suggest that inner processes and attitudes are multifaceted and influenced by many different factors. It is therefore necessary for teachers not to depend on general ideas and assumptions related to DHH learners but approach them individually based on a careful diagnosis of their values, attitudes, experiences, and previous knowledge. What comes into play here is not only the degree of the loss of hearing and the familial and educational histories, but also the personality, interests, and preferences of each individual learner.

Conclusion

The goal of this chapter was to point to some of the many aspects in which DHH foreign language learners can differ from each other. Even though prelingually profoundly deaf learners can be expected to share some characteristics based on their hearing loss, it is extremely important to avoid taking these assumptions for granted and to approach each learner individually. Besides considering the "classical" individual learning differences, factors related to DHH people's particular situations need to be taken into account.

One of the most important contributions of the research cited here is that it shows just how diverse DHH learners can be. Although their degree and onset of hearing loss (profound prelingual loss) were similar and they shared some experiences with regard to their language and reading development, they differed considerably based on other factors. The primary factor was the hearing status of their parents, which impacted their early language development. Other areas of difference included the parents' support of their early language development, their experiences with language instruction at school, and their attitudes, habits, interests, motivations, and personality. It has been shown that for instruction to be effective, it must reflect learners' individual differences and build on their existing knowledge (Chamot & O'Malley, 1994).

References

Bochner, J. H., & Albertini, J. A. (1996). Language varieties in the deaf population and their acquisition by children and adults. In M. Strong (Ed.), *Language learning and deafness* (pp. 3–48). Cambridge: Cambridge University Press.

Chamot, A. U., & O'Malley, J. M. (1994). Instructional approaches and teaching procedures. In K. S. Urbschat & R. Pritchard (Eds.), *Kids come in all languages: Reading instruction for ESL students*. Newark, DE: International Reading Association.

Csizér, K., Kontra, E. H., & Piniel, K. (2015). An investigation of the self-related concepts and foreign language motivation of young deaf and hard-of-hearing learners in Hungary. *Studies in Second Language Learning and Teaching, 5*(2), 229–249.

DeKeyser, R. M. (2000). The robustness of critical period effects in second language acquisition. *Studies in Second Language Acquisition, 22*(4), 499–533.

Domagała-Zyśk, E. (2015). Teaching English as a second language to deaf and hard-of-hearing students. In M. Marschark & P. E. Spencer (Eds.), *The Oxford handbook of deaf studies in language* (pp. 231–244). New York, NY: Oxford University Press.

Domagała-Zyśk, E. and Kontra, E. H. (2016). *English as a foreign language for deaf and hard-of-hearing persons: Challenges and strategies*. Newcastle upon Tyne: Cambridge Scholars.

Dörnyei, Z. (2005). *The psychology of the language learner; Individual differences in second language acquisition*. Mahwah, NJ: Lawrence Erlbaum.

Dörnyei, Z., & Skehan, P. (2003). Individual differences in second language learning. In C. J. Doughty & M. H. Long (Eds.), *The handbook of second language acquisition* (pp. 589–630). Oxford: Blackwell.

Easterbrooks, S. R., & Beal-Alvarez, J. (2013). *Literacy instruction for students who are deaf and hard of hearing*. New York: Oxford University Press.

Ellis, N. C., & Larsen-Freeman, D. (2006). Language emergence: Implications for applied linguistics. Introduction to the Special Issue. *Applied Linguistics, 27,* 558–589.

Ellis, R. (2004). Individual differences in second language learning. In A. Davies & C. Elder (Eds.), *The handbook of applied linguistics* (pp. 525–551). Oxford: Blackwell Publishing.

Emmorey, K. (2002). *Language, cognition, and the brain; Insights from sign language research.* Mahwah, NJ: Lawrence Erlbaum and Associates.

Gadamer, H. G. (1966). Man and language. In D. E. Linge (Ed.), *Philosophical hermeneutics: Hans-Georg Gadamer* (pp. 59–68). Los Angeles, CA: University of California Press.

Herzig, M. P. (2009). *Understanding the motivation of deaf adolescent Latino struggling readers.* [Unpublished doctoral dissertation]. Retrieved from ProQuest Dissertations and Theses Database.

Horáková, R. (2006). Úvod do surdopedie. In J. Pipeková (Ed.), *Kapitoly ze speciální pedagogiky* (2nd ed., pp. 127–143). Brno, Czech Republic: Masaryk University.

Jia, L. (2008). Learning a language, best age. In J. M. González (Ed.), *Encyclopedia of bilingual education* (Vol. 1, pp. 520–523). Thousand Oaks, CA: SAGE Publications.

Kellett Bidoli, C. J., & Ochse, E. (Eds.). (2008). *English in international deaf communication.* Bern, Germany: Peter Lang.

Knoors, H. (2015). Foundations for language development in deaf children and the consequences for communication choices. In M. Marschark & P. E. Spencer (Eds.), *The Oxford handbook of deaf studies in language* (pp. 19–31). New York, NY: Oxford University Press.

Krahulcová, B. (2003). *Komunikace sluchově postižených.* Praha, Czech Republic: Karolinum Univerzity Karlovy.

Larsen-Freeman, D., & Cameron, L. (2008). *Complex systems and applied linguistics.* Oxford: Oxford University Press.

Macurová, A. (1998). Naše řeč? *Naše řeč, 81*(4), 179–188. Retrieved from http://nase-rec.ujc.cas.cz/archiv.php?art=7457

Macurová, A., & Hanáková, D. (2011). Chyby v psané češtině českých neslyšících. *Speciální pedagogika, 21*(3), 178–190. Retrieved from http://dspace.specpeda.cz/handle/0/229

Marschark, M., Paivio, A., Spencer, L. J., Durkin, A., Borgna, G., Convertino, C., & Machmer, E. (2017). Don't assume deaf students are visual learners. *Journal of Developmental and Physical Disabilities, 29*(1), 153–171. https://doi.org/10.1007/s10882-016-9494-0

Marschark, M., Sarchet, T., Convertino, C. M., Borgna, G., Morrison, C., & Remelt, S. (2012). Print exposure, reading habits, and reading achievement among deaf and hearing college students. *Journal of Deaf Studies and Deaf Education, 17*(1), 61–74.

Marschark, M., Spencer, L. J., Durkin, A., Borgna, G., Convertino, C., Machmer, E., . . . & Trani, A. (2015). Understanding language, hearing status, and visual-spatial skills. *Journal of Deaf Studies and Deaf Education, 20*(4), 310–330.

McAnally, P. L., Rose, S., & Quigley, S. P. (2007). *Reading practices with deaf learners.* Austin, TX: Pro-Ed.

Mole, J., McColl, H., & Vale, M. (2005). *Deaf and multilingual: A practical guide to teaching and supporting deaf learners in foreign language classes.* Derbyshire, UK: Direct Learn Services.

Najvar, P., & Hanušová, S. (2010). Fenomén času v učení se cizím jazykům. *Studia Paedagogica, 15*(1), 65–84. Retrieved from https://www.phil.muni.cz/journals/index.php/studia-paedagogica/article/view/98.

Newport, E. (1990). Maturational constraints on language learning. *Cognitive Science, 14*(1), 11–28.

Oxford, R. L. (1990). *Language learning strategies: What every teacher should know.* Boston, MA: Heinle & Heinle.

Paul, P. V. (2009). *Language and deafness* (4th ed.). Boston, MA: Jones & Bartlett.

Rudy, J. W. (2008). *The neurobiology of learning and memory.* Sunderland, MA: Sinauer Associates, Inc. Publishers.

Sandler, W., & Lillo-Martin, D. (2002). Natural sign languages. In M. Aronoff & J. Rees-Miller (Eds.), *The handbook of linguistics* (pp. 533–562). Oxford: Blackwell Publishing.

Sedláčková, J. (2016). Challenges of reading comprehension development of deaf learners in the foreign language classroom: putting theory into practice. In E. Kontra & E. Domagała-Zyśk (Eds.), *English as a foreign language for deaf and hard of hearing persons: Challenges and strategies* (pp. 109–134). Newcastle-upon-Tyne: Cambridge Scholars Publishing Ltd.

Sparks, R., & Ganschow, L. (1993). The impact of native language learning problems on foreign language learning: Case study illustrations of the linguistic coding deficit hypothesis. *The Modern Language Journal, 77*(1), 58–74.

Spencer, P. E., & Marschark, M. (2010). *Evidence-based practice in educating deaf and hard-of-hearing students.* Oxford: Oxford University Press.

World Health Organization. (2012). *Community based rehabilitation.* Retrieved from www.who.int/pbd/deafness/news/CBREarHearingCare.pdf?ua=1

6 Deaf schoolchildren, adolescents, and adults on methods and strategies that work for them when learning foreign languages

Edit H. Kontra

Introduction

Foreign language teachers of special needs (SN) learners have to work hard to find appropriate methods, techniques, and strategies to help their students achieve success in acquiring a second or third language. Experience shows that most teachers develop their methods and materials on their own during the course of teaching. For a researcher it is an interesting question to ask whether the students, if given a chance, would want to be taught by the same methods their teachers have developed for them. The present study takes a look at this issue from the perspective of the learners and lets their voices be heard directly. Deaf and hard of hearing (DHH) schoolchildren, adolescents, and adults speak about their language learning experiences and voice their opinion about teaching methods, techniques, and activities that they like and dislike in foreign language (FL) learning.

The job of all language teachers of SN learners is hindered by the fact that books on FL teaching methodology are written with mainstream students and their teachers in mind (e.g. Harmer, 2015; Scrivener, 2011; Ur, 2012), and little or no attention is paid to students with learning difficulties or sensory impairments. On the other hand, books that do put the SN learner in focus are hardly ever concerned with the teaching and learning of a FL. The same can be said about electronic sources available on the Internet: they deal with either special needs learners or FL education but seldom both. Teachers and trainees with an emerging interest in SN language learners have a hard time finding self-study materials that provide insight into the nature of particular special educational needs (SEN) and, at the same time, also help them develop their pedagogical knowledge and teaching skills.

Language teaching methodology for Deaf and severely hard-of-hearing learners

It follows from the previous section that teachers of Deaf[1] and hard of hearing language learners find themselves in an especially disadvantaged situation. SN education as such is not at the forefront of attention in general, and for FL teachers of the Deaf specifically, there is very little support; there are no special training programs and there is no comprehensive methodology handbook to consult. Research on Deaf language learning is concerned with the acquisition of sign languages and the teaching and learning of the hearing majority's spoken language and literacy skills; the issue of teaching and learning FLs is given no (Gregory, Knight, McCracken, Powers, & Watson, 2012; Marschark, 1997; Marschark, Lang, & Albertini, 2002), or only a little attention (Marschark & Spencer, 2016). Fleming's (2008) observation that "second language teaching was not included in Teacher of the Deaf training" in Britain (pp. 137–138) holds internationally (cf. Bedoin, 2011). Language teachers have to resort to building up their knowledge in a piecemeal fashion, drawing from parts of chapters and websites (cf. Eilers-crandall, 2008). The practical guide by Mole, McCall, and Vale (2008), or edited volumes such as those by Kellett Bidoli and Ochse (2008), Domagała-Zyśk (2013), or Domagała-Zyśk and Kontra (2016), are attempts to fill a gap that is still substantial.

The most fundamental source that can be recommended for a language teacher who is new to the Deaf context is the booklet by Mole et al. (2008). The usefulness of this practical guide is ensured by the authors' years of experience working with Deaf learners. This thin but content-rich volume discusses deafness, hearing aids, and the various means of communication that can be used in educating language learners with different degrees of hearing loss. It offers advice and teaching tips for developing the four skills-reading, writing, listening comprehension, and speaking-, planning lessons, and creating a syllabus. With the help of short quotes and personal accounts, it offers an insider's perspective of the difficulties Deaf language learners have to face in a hearing world.

Most journal articles and book chapters that give practical advice to teachers also build on the personal teaching experience of the researcher. Cawthorn and Chambers (1993) offer practical advice on making French and German as FLs accessible to Deaf learners by doing a great deal of reading with them, providing written support, using videos, employing plenty of repetition, and adjusting the overall pace of the lessons. Acknowledging that spoken English has little relevance in the lives of Deaf university students from abroad, Fleming (2008) emphasizes the importance of using British Sign Language (BSL) as the language of instruction accompanied by detailed handouts including the written translations of material that is signed during the English lesson. Eilers-crandall (2008) reports on implementing a learner-centered approach by inviting her English as a foreign language (EFL) students to suggest topics and texts to use in a non-fiction reading class in which she also let them select the vocabulary they needed in order to understand the texts. Sedláčková (2016) recommends cognitive and metacognitive strategies that she used effectively to develop the EFL reading skills of college students. In the same volume, Domagała-Zyśk (2016) introduces a handful of techniques she generated to teach advanced English vocabulary to Polish university students. Pritchard (2013) discusses the usefulness of introducing BSL to Norwegian pupils as "a highly motivating starting point" (p. 129) to learning spoken English, which of course presupposes that the EFL teachers also receive training in BSL. In a similar vein, Piñar, Ammons, and Montenegro (2008) argue for the introduction of Costa Rican Sign Language in a course of written Spanish for American Deaf students.

All of the aforementioned publications contain language teaching methods and activities that the authors have used successfully with their own DHH students. However, the language teachers' experiences constitute only one side of the coin. In order to get the full picture, it is necessary to look at the other side as well and find out how students feel about various approaches and tasks. The present study attempts to give insight into this missing aspect of Deaf FL learning. As a small contribution to our knowledge about the FL learning of DHH people, this chapter presents approaches, methods, and activities that teenage and adult language learners mentioned in individual interviews about their experiences in special schools, mainstream education, and language courses for adults in Hungary.

Research context

The data in this study come from two projects carried out by a small team of researchers at the Department of English Applied Linguistics at Eötvös Loránd University (ELTE) in Budapest, Hungary between 2006–2010 and 2012–2015 respectively. The first project[2] entailed the collection of both quantitative and qualitative data from DHH adults about their previous language learning experiences at school, in higher education, and in other programs (for details see Kontra, 2013, and Kontra & Csizér, 2013). The second project[3] was conducted at schools for children with SEN in Hungary and involved a survey as well as individual interviews (Csizér, Kontra, & Piniel, 2015; Kontra, Csizér, & Piniel, 2014; Kontra, Csizér, & Piniel, 2015). In each project, the use of Hungarian Sign Language (HSL) as the medium of instruction turned out to be a central issue. (For further research at ELTE see Csizér & Kontra, 2020.)

Advocating the use of sign language in Deaf education might seem a thing of the past for many, but in countries with strong oralist traditions these efforts are still on-going. Hungary is one such country. In a recent nationwide survey of 90 teachers at SN schools, there were only four hard of hearing and three Deaf teachers. The rest were hearing colleagues, and only 62% of them reported having at least some knowledge of HSL (Csuhai, Henger, Mongyi, & Perlusz, 2009). Moreover, most of them rated their proficiency level as only intermediate, in other words, not sufficient for deploying it as the medium of instruction in Deaf and severely hard of hearing groups. Csuhai et al. also mention that, in most cases, this is likely to entail sign-supported Hungarian – signs expressed using the grammatical order of spoken Hungarian – rather than natural HSL. This is possible because the special schools for DHH children apply the auditory-verbal approach, a form of oralism that de-emphasizes speech-reading and concentrates on the development and use of residual hearing (Csuhai et al., 2009). The case of FL teachers is somewhat special, since they do not necessarily have a degree in special education; having a qualification for teaching a FL is sufficient for getting hired as a language teacher in a special school for the Deaf and hard of hearing. In our second research project, we found that out of 10 language teachers, only six had special education training, and only two of those six were proficient HSL users (Piniel, Kontra, & Csizér, 2016).

In the following section, basic principles, methods, techniques, and activities are presented based on the qualitative data collected in individual interviews with 23 Deaf (n=18) and severely hard of hearing (n=5) adults in our first project (hereafter *adult project*) and 31 students aged 14–19 at schools for Deaf and hard of hearing learners in our second project (hereafter *school project*). In the case of the adult participants, the interviews lasted about an hour and included accounts of past school experiences as well as more recent involvement in FL courses or self-study, mainly of English and German. The interviews with Deaf and severely hard of hearing schoolboys and schoolgirls were shorter, lasting about 30 minutes each and eliciting data about preferred and dispreferred FL (mainly English) teaching and learning activities in and out of class. The interviews were conducted with the help of a sign language interpreter, but a few of the hard of hearing participants preferred to respond to the questions in spoken Hungarian. There was one student in the school sample with a CI, but there were no CIs among the adults. The interviews were both audio and video recorded with the participants' permission and were subjected to qualitative analysis using the software MAXQDA. Quotes from the Hungarian interview transcripts are cited in the author's English translation. In order to preserve the anonymity of the participants, they are identified by codes in which "A" stands for adults and "S" for students, and a number stands for the individual (e.g. A-17, S-23).

Methods received well by the students

The use of written support

One of the basic principles mentioned positively by both the adult and the school sample is the provision of *all* information in writing. This can be done by the teacher distributing handouts as recommended by Fleming (2008); writing on the chalkboard; and/or using old-fashioned overhead slides, a laptop with a projector, or an interactive whiteboard. One of the advantages of a printed handout is its permanence; it can be taken home and used for study or revision. Another advantage is that it eases the burden of note taking on the students so they can give their full attention to the teacher's explanation. The advantage of the teacher writing on the board is that it focuses the visual attention of the whole class of usually 6–10 students on one location, and students get a sense of working together. One of our adult participants explained:

> They wrote everything on the board. The tasks were on the board. The teacher called on a student: come to the board, do the task. We could all see it. We helped each other. . . . This was very good. We were always writing. There were oral things too, but lip-reading was difficult for me.
>
> (A-7)

The danger in writing on the board is that less experienced teachers or those who are used to teaching hearing students might easily forget that with Deaf students in the group, they should not speak with their back to the class. This is why the use of an overhead projector is preferred by some teachers: they can write on the slides while facing the students. The interactive whiteboard is an excellent teaching aid because it combines the advantages of other techniques: full handouts (prepared in advance or on the spot) can be projected, written on, saved, and recalled, and after the lesson they can be sent to the computers of all the students to keep and use (cf. Nabiałek, 2013). Unfortunately, very few of the classrooms we saw during our fieldwork were equipped with this advanced technical aid.

Almost all of our adult participants, even those who had taken part in private tutoring, emphasized the importance of the teacher writing things down. One young adult recalled his hearing father starting to teach him German via writing. Later he had a one-to-one English tutor who could not use sign language and also explained everything in writing. "The sheets of paper piled up like a tower" (A-17), he said. A young woman also praised her former private English tutor for using a lot of writing. The tutor was young and inexperienced and her speech unsuitable for lip-reading, never-theless, she left positive memories in the student:

> She was very good, still a young girl but very good. She wrote every-thing down that she wanted to say because she articulated very poorly, I could not understand a thing, but she was a good teacher, she under-stood what I was saying, she could understand me completely, just I could not understand her [speech]. She kept writing, writing, and writ-ing everything down and so I could understand it. It was good.
>
> (A-15)

An adult interviewee who attended a high school for hearing students did not get this kind of help from her teacher but still managed to cope with German by having a friend make a carbon copy of all the notes she was taking in class for her. This was extremely helpful since a Deaf or severely hard of hearing person cannot listen/lip-read and take notes at the same time. A secondary school student also commented positively about her teacher explaining grammar in writing. Since the teacher could not sign, she gave her explanations in speech, but to help the Deaf students understand what she was saying she also wrote it on the board. Writing was also used by some students for asking questions. A schoolgirl with a CI said: "I do not understand when they talk, so then we communicate in writing" (S-12, Kontra et al., 2014, p. 151).

The participants related negative experiences as well. When they were taking part in integrated language classes with teachers who were not pre-pared for having a Deaf student in the group, the Deaf students seriously missed getting the information in writing: "The course started, it was dif-ficult. The teacher was only talking. I was unable to follow" (A-17). This interviewee's words describe a rather common situation wherein a school formally integrates SN students but sidelines them pedagogically. In the previous example, the teacher did not take into account the Deaf learner's needs and failed to accommodate him. The teacher appeared to expect him to adjust to the kind of teaching offered, not the other way round.

Writing as a memory strategy

Several students reported using writing for memorizing words, texts, or grammar rules. While hearing students often learn by saying and repeating things out loud, our DHH participants employed reading and writing. One 9th grader used writing to learn words first and then sentences. He said that writing things down helped him memorize them and described his personal learning strategy as follows: "When there is something I do not know, I

write it down and later I get it out again and may write it several times"
(S-19). A Deaf girl in a 7th grade group reported this:

s: First I read it, then I write down what I have to learn, and I compare.
I: What do you compare with what?
s. My written text with what I have read.

(S-23)

Some students had elaborate systems for memorizing material for an in-
class test with firm suggestions about how many times one should read a
word or sentence or how many times one should write it down. When asked
about how he memorized material so that he would know it by heart, a boy
in the 8th grade responded as follows:

s: Well you could read it five or ten times, but following that you must
    write.
I: So you mean you copy it?
s: You must write it down from memory, what you have read, that.
I: So you read the text five times, then you put it aside and write down from
    memory what you have read?
s: Yes. This is what we usually do.

(S-13)

The important element in these two excerpts is that the students deliberately
do not *copy* the material. By reading it several times, usually a fixed number
of times, they try to hold it in their memory, and then they write it down
from memory for practice.

Communicative tasks

Contemporary course books and supplementary language teaching materials available internationally tend to apply the communicative approach and
are filled with oral communication tasks. Pair work, however, can cause
problems. As Cawthorn and Chambers (1993) remark, "[e]ach pupil needs
to know in advance the question which is to be asked and the answer which
is expected. Communication with any spontaneity is well nigh impossible" (p. 48). Our adult participants nevertheless reported having fun with
rehearsing and acting out course book dialogues. If they did it orally, they
usually supported their speech with HSL. As a young girl explained: "I
cannot sign in English; I just said the words in English and used Hungarian
Sign Language. . . . If I only used speech, well, that would not be understood" (A-3).

Another student recalled that with one of his former teachers, they used to practise dialogues in writing. For controlled practice, the teacher wrote a one-sided dialogue on the board and the students took turns adding the missing lines. For free practice, they formed pairs and communicated with each other in writing: one of them wrote a question, and the other responded, and so a complete conversation developed.

In our school sample, the interview transcripts did not contain much information about oral activities or situational tasks used in class. However, several students told us that in their free time they were frequent users of online chat and tried to establish contact with foreign peers. Their level of English did not allow them to have complex conversations, but they tried to use the few phrases they knew for introducing themselves and finding out about others. If they did not understand something, they used an online translation tool.

The role of speech and pronunciation

The fact that most of the participants had language teachers who could not use HSL and applied writing as the main means of communication, raises the question of whether the students were interested in learning to speak in the FL and finding out how words are pronounced, and whether they wanted to practise articulation. Our participants' opinions varied in this respect and were heavily influenced by previous classroom experiences. For adults who had learnt German or Russian, languages with close sound-symbol matching, pronunciation was not an issue. For learners of English, a language with little sound-symbol correspondence, not only speaking but also comprehension via lip-reading constituted a problem. When encountering new lexical items in English, they wanted their teachers to give them the pronunciation of each word, to demonstrate what it looked like on his or her lips, as well as transcribe it using Hungarian spelling instead of the International Phonetic Alphabet (IPA) which teachers are taught to use in hearing groups. One of our hard of hearing adult participants was so interested in learning to speak in English that she suggested schools should provide speech therapy sessions not only in Hungarian but in English as well. She explained that even if she checked the phonetic transcription of new words in a dictionary, without help she could not be sure that she was reading it out correctly, and if she mispronounced the word, she would not be understood. Another adult participant who had already spent some time in Britain criticized a popular English course book for not providing the phonetic transcription of words. He said he would need it for recognizing the word on the lips of interlocutors.

Most participants, however, tended to only make a note of the oral form but memorized the item according to its written form, still using the

Hungarian pronunciation. Several students reported memorizing new words this way, rehearsing them mentally without sounding them out, as illustrated by the following example:

S: Without sound.
I: You hear it inside?
S: Yes.
I: And what do you hear? Do you hear L-O-V-E and L-I-K-E, or [lʌv] and [laik]?
S: That I cannot. Only as it is written.

(E-21)

Lip reading in English was invariably described as difficult, and those who had no residual hearing refused to attempt oral communication. A young woman explained: "I cannot speak; I do not hear anything; it is hopeless" (A-9). Whether someone attempts to speak or not also depends on the setting. Deaf students might feel more confident in a group of DHH peers than in an integrated class. Special schools for DHH children and adolescents provide a sheltered environment where students can feel more secure. One hard of hearing student in the 9th grade expressed his worries about using speech in real life: "I would have liked to try communicating, but I am very much afraid, I do not know how it would work out with a stranger, I am afraid of that" (S-19, Kontra et al., 2014, p. 10).

Another young man reported his experience in his former secondary school, which was a mainstream school:

> At first I attempted to rely on lip-reading but I found it quite impossible to follow what was going on; besides, the others were laughing at me. If everybody is Deaf and the teacher is patient, that is different, but I was with hearing students and I could not pronounce [English]. I did give it a try but everybody was staring at me. There was some ridiculing as well, so I gave it up. I stopped trying.

(A-8)

In our school sample, one of the 8th grade students was worried about continuing learning English in a high school for IT for the same reason: "They speak a lot there and what if I do not understand what they are learning about and then sometimes I try to also say something? I am a bit worried" (S-20). This would not be a problem if mainstream schools that integrate SN students prepared their teachers thoroughly to accommodate these learners and if teachers discussed with the other students how they can support classmates who formerly attended a SN school.

Reading

For Deaf FL learners, reading is the most important skill to acquire. As Sedláčková (2016) asserts, for Deaf persons "foreign language input as well as their actual use of the language primarily involves the written form" (p. 110). Reading is what they do when they surf the Internet, look for information in printed or online sources, exchange e-mails or chat with a foreigner, or watch a DVD with FL subtitles. Practising reading comprehension in and out of class is therefore an essential component of FL acquisition.

Investigating the relationship between American Sign Language (ASL) skills and the ability to read in English in a US context, Padden and Ramsey (2000) point out that for a signing child, learning to read must be doubly complicated since they do not have direct access to the spoken language, and "presumably do not use, at least not efficiently, sounding out processes that might help them learn to read" (p. 165). We can assume that this difficulty is multiplied in the case of a Deaf person trying to read English as a FL, which for them is a third language (L3). Furthermore, it is well documented that the limited linguistic competence of deaf persons, including limited vocabulary and structural awareness in the national spoken language (L2), can constitute a major obstacle to their reading development in an L3. How far Deaf language learners are capable of transferring their limited L2 reading skills to their L3 may vary from person to person.

In our two projects, we encountered different types of readers demonstrating varying levels of motivation to apply their reading skills to real life reading tasks. One of the adult participants recalled how he became fascinated with comic books as a young boy. In those days, comic books were only available in English, so at the age of 9 he started reading and collecting them:

> I will tell you frankly, in my childhood, the first comic book in my life was not a Hungarian comic book, and I used to understand what was going on from the pictures, from the actions, . . . and until this day I buy comic books, but now that I know English better, I can understand from the text up to about 70% what it is all about. . . . Batman, Spiderman, Superman, they have different titles but this is what I like . . . always in English.

(A-5)

At first, he managed to figure out the meaning of the short texts in the speech bubbles by looking at the drawings, and later he started checking words in dictionaries. At the time of the interview, he was 29 and still collecting comics, sometimes also sharing them and translating them into Hungarian for his friends if necessary.

A hard of hearing female participant preferred using dual-language readers to sustain her English knowledge. She explained how these booklets had several advantages:

> [T]here are these good little books with the text in English on one side and in Hungarian on the other side, and with these you can practice [the language] really well, because if there is something you do not understand, you can easily check it; you do not need to search for it in a dictionary.
>
> (A-21)

Since dual-language readers are usually graded, comprehension is made easy by the use of simple structures and a limited set of vocabulary items.

The reading of professional texts was typical of those adult participants who were working in IT-related jobs. In their case, encountering English texts and reading them for gist or some specific information happened on a daily basis. Using the electronic dictionary to aid comprehension was common in both the adult and the school sample. The participants in this latter group also frequently mentioned that instead of trying to work out the meaning using contextual clues, they resorted to feeding the text into a popular translator program. This may work well as a quick aid but, unfortunately, is a less useful strategy to aid FL acquisition in the long run.

When translating a foreign text for comprehension, an intriguing question is what language the text should be translated into. Several studies mention that native sign language users tend to think in sign. Some of our own research participants were sometimes observed signing to themselves while reading something, for instance the data collection questionnaire they were filling out for the project, and some of them confirmed in the interviews that they would frequently *sign mentally*, without moving their hands. An adult female participant who was born deaf and could not communicate in any language until the age of 6 told us in her interview how she visualized what she was reading:

> [W]hen I read a Hungarian text, I see the picture through Hungarian Sign Language, as I do not hear it, but like a movie I see it in front of me. A similar thing happens if I read an English text; the text appears in ASL. If there is a dialogue, I imagine two Deaf persons signing to each other. I do not hear anything, nothing. It is just pictures, pictures and pictures and sign language. These two.
>
> (A-9)

This finding is in accordance with the assertion made by Piñar et al. (2008) that connections made between signs and written words "enhance vocabulary retention (both spelling and meaning) and global text comprehension" (p. 141). A girl in our school sample who identified herself as Deaf and was learning English from a teacher who used HSL in the English class also talked about the use of this strategy:

> When I am reading a text, one word after the other, I translate it to myself through sign language. I mean, I am not going to sign, because I do not want everybody to stare at me, so I translate it all into sign language mentally. I imagine it and so.
>
> (S-5)

This strategy can be utilized by FL teachers when doing reading comprehension tasks in the classroom. Easterbrooks (2010) points out that in the case of children who "do not read orally, fluent signed renderings of text can provide teachers with information regarding their students' reading comprehension" (p. 115). This approach was used by an English teacher of a few of our adult participants. They recalled reading texts in class and taking turns in signing the meaning of sentences as a positive experience:

I: Did you read texts in class, English texts?
S: Yes, yes. We had to sound out the text and sign at the same time. And the teacher tried to correct us. Yes, because when I sign, the teacher can see that I understand, she sees that I understand what it is about. If not, then she sees that I do not understand. So she required that as we read, we should sign what it is about.

> (A-3)

This activity can only work under the following two conditions: firstly, the participants should sit in a circle or semi-circle so that they each have a good view of the others; and secondly, each student must be a fluent signer, including those for whom sign language is not the first or preferred language. If in a group of students with mixed levels of hearing loss there is a person who prefers speaking, the Deaf students cannot follow what he or she is saying or discussing with the teacher, and they feel left out.

Use of sign language

The use of HSL was supported by all participants both in the adult and in the school project (for details see Kontra & Csizér, 2013; Kontra et al., 2014). Due to their age, the adult participants had more varied experiences of being taught with or without the use of sign language than the boys and girls at school, many of whom had only encountered one or two language teachers during their lifetime and had little or no experience with HSL in FL education. Nevertheless, the reasons for preferring teaching methods that involve sign language were found to be similar across both groups and can be categorized as follows: barrier-free information transfer; explaining grammar; approximating 'Deaf thinking'; and enhanced teacher-student rapport.

Several participants made it clear that understanding spoken language was very difficult for them. Much of the information got lost and what they managed to comprehend via lip-reading were only fragments that had to be put together like pieces of a puzzle. The chances of misunderstanding or misinterpretation were considerable. This led to frustration and the loss of motivation, as explained by one of the adult interviewees: "If a plain hearing person comes to a Deaf school and starts teaching English without using sign language, that is very difficult. That turns you off completely" (A-16). The need for getting the meaning in sign language was self-evident for some of the teenage participants whose teacher was proficient in HSL: "Because I am Deaf. This is what I need for communication," one of them explained (S-25, Kontra et al., 2014, p. 151).

Sign language use is considered especially important for the explanation of grammar. In this case, sign language is not only the medium through which teacher and students understand each other but also a reference point. Students found that teachers who were sign language users and were aware of how sign languages work had better ways of explaining FL grammar than those who had no signing skills. A few of the adult participants had a chance to get help with English through ASL and found it extremely useful. A young woman explained how her Deaf American acquaintances helped her:

If I had a problem, some grammar or something, I asked them, and they explained it, and it worked. I understood quickly. When I tried to learn it from books, it was hard. I forgot. When they explained it once or twice in sign language, I understood it right away. Just as the hearing learn English fast via the auditory channel, I learn visually, via sign language.

(A-9)

Comments such as these led the interviewers to the question of whether the participants would prefer Deaf FL teachers to hearing ones. The question was strictly hypothetical since at the time of our data collection there were no qualified Deaf FL teachers in the country. A young man who seemed to be the most talented language learner in the whole adult sample thought that hearing teachers who can sign would be good but Deaf FL teachers would be even better because they would understand Deaf thinking and they would know what to link the new material to in the Deaf student's mind. He thought that finding mental connections was essential: "If you do not have this, it is hopeless" (A-2).

Last but not least, the use of sign language in class was considered important by our participants for establishing good teacher-student relations. Even if a teacher arrived at an SN school without any knowledge of HSL but showed interest, made an effort to learn fingerspelling, and tried to pick up signs from the students or maybe even enrolled in an HSL course, it was much appreciated by all. Besides having practical benefits, it was an indication of acceptance and a positive attitude, and a way of showing genuine care.

Conclusion

One of the positive conclusions we are able to draw from the two research projects is that indeed we need not worry about whether Deaf and severely hard of hearing persons are capable of learning foreign languages (Mole et al., 2008): data gathered from the two Hungarian samples provide ample evidence that they are, and contribute to the findings of researchers in other contexts. We can also see that there is still plenty of work to do to find out how these learners can be taught best and how their special needs could be better catered for so that they can achieve their potential.

Unfortunately, the circumstances in present-day Hungary are far from ideal for SN learners. Deaf students need plenty of written support and this could be provided at a much higher quality if classrooms were equipped with modern technology, with projectors or interactive whiteboards. Teachers, particularly those who teach languages in integrated settings, would need teaching assistants to give individual support to the Deaf student in class. This would also require training programs for such staff, including at least some FL component.

Since children and adolescents like spending time online, providing free Internet access on the school premises would make it possible for language learners to use web-based sources to practise their language skills, search for school-related materials, or just play language games. Schools could also invest in sets of graded readers and simple storybooks so that students can be introduced to reading for pleasure in a FL.

It is evident that teachers at Deaf schools should be proficient signers so that they can conduct lessons in HSL and ensure barrier-free information transfer. This also enables them to use sign language as a reference point when explaining FL vocabulary and structure. Further research is necessary to explore how to incorporate foreign sign languages in the FL education process so that it supports the acquisition of the foreign spoken language, for example, using ASL to support the learning of English.

In the past few years, much has been said about providing SN learners with equal opportunities in education and lifelong learning, but little has been achieved. This goal can only be realized if educational policy makers work on ensuring appropriate facilities and training, and if governments allocate a sufficient budget for this.

Notes

1 We follow the tradition of spelling *Deaf* with a capital 'D' to denote people who share a sign language as well as distinct cultural values and consider themselves a linguistic and cultural minority. In contrast, the word *deaf* spelled with a lower-case 'd' refers to the audiological condition (i.e. a disability).
2 Supported by a grant from the Hungarian National Bureau of Research and Technology (NKTH B2 2006–0010).
3 This work was supported by the Hungarian Scientific Research Fund under Grant OTKA-K-105095.

References

Bedoin, D. (2011). English teachers of deaf and hard-of-hearing students in French schools: Needs, barriers and strategies. *European Journal of Special Needs Education, 26*(2), 159–175. https://doi.org/10.1080/08856257.2011.563605

Cawthorn, I., & Chambers, G. (1993, March). The special needs of the deaf foreign language learner. *Language Learning Journal, 7*, 47–49.

Csizér, K., & Kontra, E. H. (2020). Foreign language learning characteristics of deaf and severely hard-of-hearing students. *The Modern Language Journal, 104*(1), 233–249.

Csizér, K., Kontra, E. H., & Piniel, K. (2015). An investigation of the self-related concepts and foreign language motivation of young deaf and hard-of-hearing learners in Hungary. *Studies in Second Language Learning and Teaching, 5*(2), 229–249.

Csuhai, S., Henger. K., Mongyi, P., & Perlusz, A. (2009). *„Siket gyermekek kétnyelvű oktatásának lehetőségei és korlátai" című kutatás eredményei. Zárótanulmány*. Budapest: Fogyatékos Személyek Esélyegyenlőségéért Közalapítvány. Retrieved from www.fszk.hu/mjp/szakmai-anyagok/Siket-gyermekek-ketnyelvu-oktatasanak-lehetosegei-es-korlatai-c-kutatas-eredmenyei_zarotanulmany.pdf

Domagała-Zyśk, E. (Ed.). (2013). *English as a foreign language for the deaf and hard of hearing in Europe: State of the art and future challenges*. Lublin, Poland: Wydawnictwo KUL.

Domagała-Zyśk, E. (2016). Vocabulary teaching strategies in English as a foreign language classes for deaf and hard-of-hearing students. In E. Domagała-Zyśk & E. H. Kontra (Eds.), *English as a foreign language for deaf and hard-of-hearing* persons: *Challenges and strategies* (pp. 135–152). Newcastle upon Tyne: Cambridge Scholars Publishing.

Domagała-Zyśk, E., & Kontra, E. H. (Eds.). (2016). *English as a foreign language for Deaf and hard-of-hearing persons: Challenges and strategies.* Newcastle upon Tyne: Cambridge Scholars Publishing.

Easterbrooks, S. R. (2010). Evidence-based curricula and practices that support the development of reading skills. In M. Marschark & P. E. Spencer (Eds.), *The Oxford handbook of deaf studies and deaf education* (Vol. 2, pp. 111–126). Oxford: Oxford University Press.

Eilers-crandall, K. (2008). Evaluating English teaching materials to identify factors that maximize deaf students' success. In D. Janáková (Ed.), *Teaching English to deaf and hard-of-hearing students at secondary and tertiary levels of education in the Czech Republic* (2nd ed., pp. 98–108). Prague, Czech Republic: VIP Books.

Fleming, J. (2008). How should we teach deaf learners? Teaching English as a written language to deaf European students. In C. J. Kellett Bidoli & E. Ochse (Eds.), *English in international deaf communication* (pp. 123–153). Bern, Switzerland: Peter Lang.

Gregory, S., Knight, P., McCracken, W., Powers, S., & Watson, L. (2012). *Issues in deaf education* (2nd ed.). New York: David Fulton.

Harmer, J. (2015). *The practice of English language teaching* (4th ed.). Harlow, UK: Pearson Longman.

Kellett Bidoli, C. J., & Ochse, E. (Eds.). (2008). *English in international deaf communication.* Bern, Switzerland: Peter Lang.

Kontra, E. H. (2013). Language learning against the odds: retrospective accounts by four deaf adults. In E. Domagała-Zyśk (Ed.), *English as a foreign language for deaf and hard-of-hearing persons in Europe: State of the art and future challenges* (pp. 93–111). Lublin, Poland: Wydawnictwo KUL.

Kontra, E. H., & Csizér, K. (2013). An investigation into the relationship of foreign language learning motivation and sign language use among deaf and hard of hearing Hungarians. *International Review of Applied Linguistics (IRAL), 51*(1), 1–22. https://doi.org/10.1515/iral-2013-masthead1

Kontra, E. H., Csizér, K., & Piniel, K. (2014). The challenge for deaf students to learn foreign languages in special needs schools. *European Journal of Special Needs Education, 30*(2), 141–155. https://doi.org/10.1080/08856257.2014.986905

Kontra, E. H., Csizér, K., & Piniel, K. (2015). Teaching and learning foreign languages in Hungarian schools for the hearing impaired: A nationwide study. *Proceedings of ICED 2015* Athens, Greece, 6–9 July. Retrieved from www.deaf.elemedu.upatras.gr/index.php/iced-2015-proceedings

Marschark, M. (1997). *Raising and educating a deaf child.* Oxford: Oxford University Press.

Marschark, M., Lang, H. G., & Albertini, J. A. (Eds.). (2002). *Educating deaf students: From research to practice.* Oxford: Oxford University Press.

Marschark, M., & Spencer, P. E. (Eds.). (2016). *The Oxford handbook of deaf studies in language.* Oxford: Oxford University Press.

Mole, J., McCall, H., & Vale, M. (2008). *Deaf and multilingual: A practical guide to teaching and supporting deaf learners in foreign language classes.* Norbury, Shropshire, UK: Direct Learn Services.

Nabiałek, A. (2013). From a blackboard to an interactive whiteboard. Teaching English as a foreign language to deaf and hard of hearing students at Adam Mickiewicz University in Poznań. In E. Domagała-Zyśk (Ed.), *English as a foreign language for deaf and hard of hearing persons in Europe: State of the art and future challenges* (pp. 197–206). Lublin, Poland: Wydawnictwo KUL.

Padden, C., & Ramsey, C. (2000). American Sign Language and reading ability in deaf children. In C. Chamberlain, J. P. Morford, & R. I. Mayberry (Eds.), *Language acquisition by eye* (pp. 165–189). Mahwah, NJ: Lawrence Erlbaum Associates.

Piñar, P., Ammons, D., & Montenegro, F. (2008). Incorporating foreign sign language in foreign language instruction for deaf students: Cultural and methodological rationale. In T. Berberi, E. C. Hamilton, & I. M. Sutherland (Eds.), *Worlds apart? Disability and foreign language learning* (pp. 137–150). New Haven, CT: Yale University Press.

Piniel, K., Kontra, E. H., & Csizér, K. (2016). Foreign language teachers at schools for deaf and hard-of-hearing students. In E. Domagała-Zyśk & E. H. Kontra (Eds.), *English as a foreign language for deaf and hard of hearing persons: Challenges and strategies* (pp. 73–88). Newcastle upon Tyne: Cambridge Scholars Publishing.

Pritchard, P. (2013). Teaching of English to deaf and severely hard-of-hearing pupils in Norway. In E. Domagała-Zyśk (Ed.), *English as a foreign language for deaf and hard-of-hearing persons in Europe: State of the art and future challenges* (pp. 113–134). Lublin, Poland: Wydawnictwo KUL.

Scrivener, J. (2011). *Learning teaching: The essential guide to English language teaching* (3rd ed.). Oxford: Macmillan.

Sedláčková, J. (2016). Challenges of the reading comprehension development of deaf learners in the foreign language classroom: Putting theory into practice. In E. Domagała-Zyśk & E. H. Kontra (Eds.), *English as a foreign language for deaf and hard-of-hearing persons: Challenges and strategies* (pp. 109–133). Newcastle upon Tyne: Cambridge Scholars.

Ur, P. (2012). *A course in English language teaching* (2nd ed.). Cambridge: Cambridge University Press.

7 Adult deaf and hard of hearing people on learning English as a foreign language – international experiences and recommendations

Paulina Lewandowska

Introduction

Fluent communication in a second, third, and subsequent language is now an important skill that is useful in many areas of individuals' lives, for example, in professional, social, and educational spheres. Multilingualism may enable DHH people to "more effectively negotiate the world in which they live" (Domagała-Zyśk & Podlewska, 2019, p. 156). At the moment, society lives in a globalized, interconnected world where English has become an international lingua franca and people with hearing loss have greater opportunities to participate due to social inclusion and inclusive education.

Therefore, more and more deaf[1] and hard of hearing (DHH) people are trying to speak and understand foreign languages, and their efforts are bolstered by wider access to technical support (e.g. hearing aids, cochlear implants, FM systems, and induction loops), changes in social attitudes, and increasing awareness of researchers and educators on DHH people's communicative and linguistic abilities and predispositions. However, the barriers and challenges that they face still exist.

Accordingly, the purpose of the empirical research presented in this article is to describe the experience of acquiring English as a foreign language (EFL) for DHH students at school, using a retrospective of current users of this language. As a result, general recommendations for teachers who have DHH students in their classes are offered. This is intended to contribute to a better quality of EFL classes for DHH students, especially in mainstream schools.

Acquisition of the language – the importance of hearing and understanding

Hearing is often an important part of learning about reality (Krakowiak, 2006). Through hearing, an individual learns not only about the world around us, but also about the rules of the surrounding spoken language, through unconscious imitation of other speakers: "Linguistic knowledge manifests itself through the perception of speech, understanding people's underlying intentions and by producing and articulating their own statements and expressing their intentions" (Olempska-Wysocka, 2016, p. 116). When a child does not receive spontaneous communicative stimuli from the environment, this can restrict the level of linguistic ability that they are able to reach. A child with hearing loss commonly struggles to acquire spoken language because he or she perceives the world of sounds in a limited way, and this includes the sounds of a foreign language (Berent, 1996; Connor, Craig, Raudenbush, Heavner, & Zwolan, 2006; Domagała-Zyśk, 2014). DHH people may improve their articulation through conscious practice, often with the help of others, while hearing children have the opportunity to do this more easily and spontaneously. Furthermore, DHH people's understanding often requires "guessing the remaining parts of the sentence, which is not always possible and adequate. It is also tiring, so they need breaks and repetitions to understand the whole utterance" (Domagała-Zyśk, 2014, p. 42). Sometimes they can hear something but not understand it, because they hear only a few individual words and not the whole sentence or message.

The role of school in DHH learners' acquisition of EFL and challenges related to it

All of this makes the acquisition of a foreign language more difficult if it is done in an environment that is unfavourable for DHH people (Marschark & Spencer, 2015). Therefore, the idea of teaching a foreign language to people with hearing loss as well as the phenomenon of their use of foreign languages has been raised in the pedagogical and scientific environment from the beginning of the 20th century, and currently exists in science as a surdo-glottodidactic (Domagała-Zyśk, 2003, 2014). The needs of people with hearing loss have been noticed.

The school and teachers can play a significant role at this point in motivating DHH students to build a solid foreign language foundation. When teachers not only engage their learners, convey the knowledge competently, and provide the appropriate emotional climate, but also ensure that they have adequate expectations and approach each learner as an individual, DHH students' difficulties can often be ameliorated. The way classes are conducted, teachers' attitudes towards their students, and the methods and strategies used to adapt the activities to students' needs can all influence DHH students' acquisition of a foreign language (Csizér & Kontra, 2020; Domagała-Zyśk, 2012a).

A study on the teacher's role when working with DHH students is presented in Domagała-Zyśk (2012b). Among the foreign language teachers surveyed, all were fully qualified to teach this subject ($n = 19$), but only half were prepared to work with DHH students. These teachers applied various foreign language teaching strategies in their work effectively but struggled to communicate with their DHH students. They also applied pedagogical and therapeutic principles aimed at enabling the student's participation in the language course (e.g. positive reinforcement, visual contact, individualization of teaching, adjustment of the pace of work, and precise transmission of instructions). Although these teachers exploited visual tools, digital teaching aids were not used very often. Moreover, in the research conducted by Bedoin (2011), most of the teachers had no specific qualifications in teaching EFL and faced challenges when adapting their methods to their students' specific needs.

International studies conducted among EFL teachers at universities show that many DHH students started tertiary education without previous experience of learning to speak a foreign language, even though they spoke their national language well. During their classes, these students "communicated . . . the desire to learn to speak a foreign language" (Domagała-Zyśk, 2015, p. 37). An interesting conclusion in this research was that although these students actually improve their English proficiency during the course, in most cases they only master the basics of foreign language skills. It can be assumed that in many cases, the reason for this is that the teacher lacks a properly developed, effective form of communication with these students and modified teaching methods and techniques that meet the students' special needs.

It can be suggested that the successful acquisition of English at school has a great impact on learners' ability to cope with the challenges of the future, so a number of steps should be taken to address the barriers that DHH students face when learning languages. Dedicated centres have been established at universities to provide specialist support for DHH students who are learning foreign languages, so that they can participate in regular classes or individual sessions with an adapted program (Domagała-Zyśk, 2013).

Pedagogical and scientific literature does not sufficiently address the topic of foreign language acquisition by DHH people in mainstream schools where teachers do not have the pedagogical preparation for working with these students. The number of DHH people who attend mainstream schools continues to grow, not only because of the right to inclusive education and full participation, but also because of the increasing numbers of DHH youth across the world (World Health Organization, 2018). Therefore, this article aims to help reduce this research gap, and provide practical recommendations for teachers to apply in their classes.

Data and methods

Participants

A total of 90 DHH participants were recruited for the research and their characteristics are presented in Table 7.1. The majority of the participants were from Poland (58 people), but 18 other countries were also represented. Three participants each were from Finland, Turkey, and the Philippines; two each were from Canada,[2] Denmark, Germany, Norway, Russia, Spain, Sweden, and the Netherlands; and one each were from Bolivia, England, Hong Kong, Italy, Tunisia, Uganda, and the United States. Almost all of them used assistive devices for everyday communication: 78.9% wore hearing aids, 33.3% had cochlear implants, and 4.4% used a cros (a contralateral routing of signals hearing aid). The proportion who used devices supporting sound perception (e.g. induction loop or FM system) was 41.1%. Two participants said that they did not use any devices.

Table 7.1 Demographic background of respondents

Factors	Questionnaire				Total	
	In Polish		In English			
	Frequency	%	Frequency	%	Frequency	%
Gender						
Women	22	37,9	18	56,2	55	61
Men	36	62,1	14	43,8	35	39
Age						
. . .–25	28	48,3	7	21,9	35	38,9
26–33	25	43,1	17	53,1	42	46,7
34–41	4	6,9	7	21,9	11	12,2
42–. . .	1	1,7	1	3,1	2	2,2
Highest completed level of education						
Secondary	9	15,5	2	6,3	11	12,2
Post-secondary	4	6,9	4	12,5	8	8,9
Bachelor	12	20,7	14	43,8	26	28,9
Master	33	37,5	12	37,5	45	50
Hearing loss[3]						
Profound	36	62,1	14	43,8	50	56,6
Severe	11	19	6	18,7	17	18,9
Moderate	10	17,2	11	34,4	21	23,3
Mild	1	1,7	1	3,1	2	2,2

Materials and research design

A quantitative methodology was used to collect and analyze the data. The author created two versions of the questionnaire, one in Polish and one in English, to collect data on the participants' experiences of learning English at school.[4] Using a comprehensive questionnaire makes it possible to understand the ways in which DHH learners acquire a foreign language and provides a basis for analyzing how they apply this skill in practice, outside school walls. In the part devoted to learning English, participants were asked about the type of schools they attended, how long they learned English and at what level, their subjective assessment of the success of their learning, and their use of various extracurricular forms of English learning. There were also open questions about the barriers and challenges they faced while learning a foreign language at school.

Data collection procedure

The research used a diagnostic survey (Nowak, 2007) as a method and a standardized questionnaire as a tool, and was conducted in July 2018. The CAWI (computer-assisted web interview) technique made it possible to reach DHH people from a variety of countries. This method of data collection not only facilitated anonymity, which was especially important for participants who divulged sensitive information about their disabilities, but also helped to ensure that they were able to complete all of the necessary questions, because of the efficient navigation provided by the CAWI.

Some of the participants were the author's contacts from recent years. A request to complete the questionnaire was sent to them by Messenger, WhatsApp, and email, emphasizing that it is voluntary. The link was also shared on Facebook groups for DHH people, for example, the 'International Federation of Hard of Hearing', 'International Federation of Hard of Hearing Young People', and 'European Federation of Hard of Hearing' groups. Five of the questionnaires are omitted from this paper and will be discussed in a future publication.[5]

Results

English as a foreign language (EFL)

Most of the respondents attended mainstream schools (Figure 7.1) for *primary*, *secondary*, and *post-secondary* education (71%, 74%, and 75% respectively). A few people indicated that they attended two or more types of school at different stages of education.

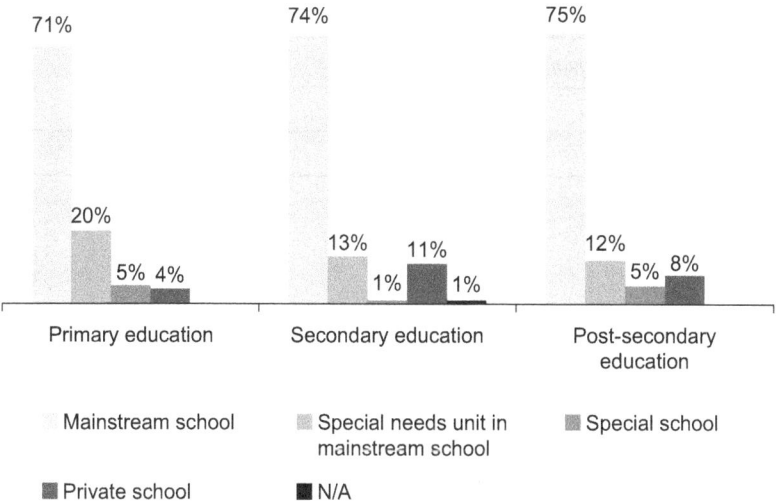

Figure 7.1 Type of school at each stage of education

The duration of English language learning differed widely among the participants. Some of them had just started studying English, while others had more than 20 years of experience. The results were grouped into five categories (Table 7.2).

Over a quarter of all respondents (25.6%) had achieved a command of English at the intermediate level (B1), and slightly smaller proportions had attained the levels of upper-intermediate (B2–22.2%) and advanced (C1–18.9%). Pre-intermediate learners made up 14.4% of the total. Only 10% of respondents were proficient (C2) and 8.9% were beginners (A1). Some participants were able to acquire more than one foreign language. Over half (59%) of the participants confirmed that they know other languages, including German (26 people), Spanish (12), French (10), and Russian (8).

Learning English

The respondents were also asked to evaluate the effectiveness of their EFL classes in retrospect, by reflecting on their current experiences of using English. Their opinions were divided. Forty percent of them gave a neutral evaluation, while slightly fewer offered positive (35.5%) or negative (24.5%) evaluations. They often spent many hours learning the language and took advantage of many additional opportunities to avoid lagging

Table 7.2 Years of learning English

| Years | Questionnaire | | | | Total | |
| | In Polish | | In English | | | |
	Amount	%	Amount	%	Amount	%
. . .–5	7	12,1	3	9,4	10	11,1
6–10	14	24,1	11	34,4	25	27,8
11–15	22	37,9	6	18,8	28	31,1
16–20	12	20,7	9	28,1	21	23,3
21–. . .	3	5,2	3	9,4	6	6,7
Total	58	100	32	100	90	100

behind their classmates. The most frequently chosen options for additional learning were *movies and series* (48 respondents), *books* (46), *additional English textbooks* (44), and *conversations with others* (43). Other options included *websites* (31 respondents), *articles* and *blogs* (23), *music* (29), *language courses* (22), and *English tutoring* (5). One respondent emphasized that before choosing the course, she had undertaken research and exchanged emails with the organizers about how to adjust the course to her needs. Other answers included the *BBC's educational language program*, *visiting a family who lives abroad*, *playing games*, and using the *Duolingo application*. Respondents were also asked whether they took private lessons in addition to learning English at school, and 38 (42%) answered *yes*. They had also accessed *tutoring* (33 respondents), *language courses* (11), and *trips abroad* and *videoconferences with native-speakers* (6).

The respondents were asked to choose their motives for gaining and improving English. The most frequent reason was *to fulfil a school requirement* (67 respondents), followed by *to enhance professional qualifications* (44), *to understand materials (websites, books, movies) in English* (46), *to be able to go abroad* (44), and *to communicate fluently with foreigners* (49) and/or *with international friends* (44). Furthermore, 35 people said their motive was that *everyone should know additional languages*, 29 wanted to learn English *for personal satisfaction of learning a foreign language*, and 13 wanted to learn it as *a hobby*.

Apart from the motivation, participants were asked if they found pleasure in learning English. The majority (61.1%) answered that they enjoyed learning it and only 16.7% said that they did not. The remainder were not sure. Another question concerned the respondents' evaluation of the statement *learning English at school will not have as much impact as learning/using*

English during everyday contact and foreign trips; 70% of them agreed with this statement and 19% disagreed.

Using English in everyday life

Proficiency in foreign languages often depends on the frequency of using them in everyday life, and the respondents' answers about how often they use English are fairly evenly distributed among the range of options (Figure 7.2).

Nowadays, DHH people have many opportunities to use English in daily life. The three most popular options were *watching and reading English films, books, and websites* (61 respondents), *communication with international friends* (54), and *classes conducted in English at university/school* (46). They used English less frequently at *work* (42) and *home while talking to family* (31). In *others*, there were activities such as: *playing games*, *participation in thematic forums*, and *maintaining a website* chosen by 3 people. Only 26 people used English when they were abroad.

Examples of barriers and challenges that affect the acquisition of English – subjective opinions from the perspective of DHH users

The participants' responses to open questions about examples of barriers and challenges that affected their acquisition of English were sorted into several categories, to highlight the complexity of the difficulties they faced.

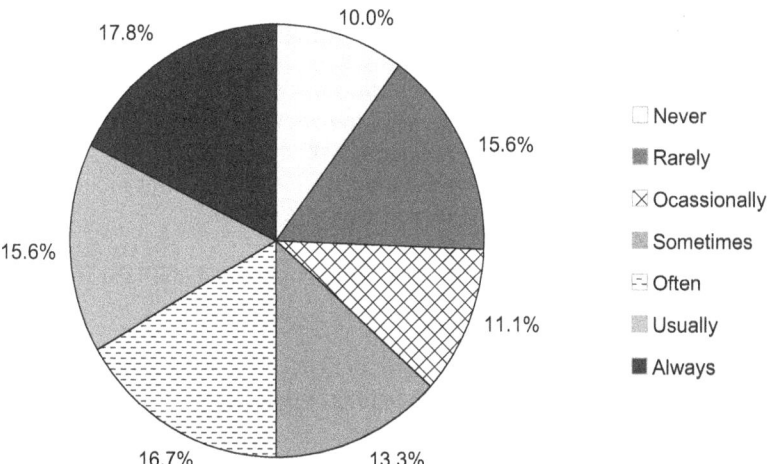

Figure 7.2 Frequency of using English in everyday life

Hearing, listening, and understanding – limitations

One of their most common difficulties was following and understanding speech or discussion only by hearing. According to the participants, the problem was often not due to poor knowledge of the language, but rather, they said:

- You can hear English speech but you can't recognize what exactly is being said (R5; R33).
- The hearing loss did not allow for physical ways to hear the words clearly and properly (R6).
- I have trouble distinguishing phonetically similar words and consolidating compound words (R19).
- It's hard to hear and distinguish the words, especially when someone speaks really fast (R51).
- There are English words with such similar pronunciations that listening is very confusing (R69).
- I still have a hard time separating words, and I see phrases as one long undecipherable word (R81).

As a result of not understanding some words, difficult situations arise in which the participants said they often lose the context of the conversation:

- By hearing only some words, I don't even get the context. I have to concentrate very hard (R74).
- I put in a lot of energy in order to catch on: "Ah! That person said that . . .!" Sometimes it takes a while, sometimes it happens after the conversation is over, but sometimes it never happens at all (R81).
- I need more time to understand the words. Sometimes I miss some parts of the conversation so I have to put the pieces of it together, and this takes time so I miss other parts (R88).
- When I can't keep up with the conversation, it's hard for me to rejoin the discussion, so I no longer participate (R90).

The need to visualize words in such situations was emphasized by some respondents:

- Hearing new words is difficult for me: I need to have them written on a piece of paper first, because sometimes I don't know if the sound I am lip-reading is p, b, or m (R2).
- A written text was needed so that I could connect with what was being said (R7).

- I didn't know what was going on. I figured it out better when it was written because I'd seen it (R70).
- To hear the differences in pronunciation I need to see new words in a written form to pronounce and remember them right (R76).

Technological and environmental barriers

A frequent issue in participants' statements was the lack of technical adaptation, which made learning English difficult or impossible for them. This included having no adapted materials or adapted tasks, and thus being expected to perform listening comprehension tasks from recordings without a transcript; access audio-visual materials without captions; and listen to a song and identify the missing words:

- I couldn't benefit from the English class, because recordings were played often (R1).
- I felt bad when I failed listening comprehension tests, but I felt excluded when I was exempted from them; they never thought of reading the transcript in front of me so I could look at them [and lip-read] (R6).
- I had to deal with situations when I failed. I got a lowered grade because of the test for listening (R9).
- Part of the exam required listening to the recorded text which was very hard for me to understand so I used to leave that part blank (R62).
- I was forced to listen to the radio for the comprehension test. It took awhile for the teacher to exempt me from them (R43).
- I was often bored when movies or recordings were played. It really was rare for me to have access to transcripts or subtitles (R90).

Among the environmental barriers that the participants faced in the classroom were: group work in a noisy environment, no induction loop to improve sound perception, too many students in the room, a large room causing reverberation, students being scattered across a large area making it impossible to see peers' faces clearly, and chairs being arranged such that some students were facing away from each other:

- I had to plan where to sit in the class so that I could see and understand as much as possible (R4).
- It is more difficult to follow in a large class; it is better for me be the only student with the teacher (R34).
- I couldn't understand my mates because they had their backs to me (I am a lip-reader) (R55).

- During group activities I was excluded because it was so loud that I couldn't hear what was going on in my group (R57).
- The words coalesced into an incomprehensible cluster of gibberish because my peers and teacher were too far away from me and my hearing aids amplified every rustle of paper, clatter of a pen, and shuffle of chairs (R66).

Lack of reasonable accommodation

- The school system did not adequately address my hearing needs such as assistive technology, clear lip-reading and reasonable accommodation in terms of extra time (R2).
- At the mainstream school I could not handle the speed which the teachers used to go through the subject, because it cost me more time to understand the subject (R8).
- There was no provision that combined English with speech therapy (bilateral speech therapy) (R71).
- There was no suitable person to show me how to pronounce correctly (R81).
- The problem sometimes was not the teacher's lack of experience, but more his lack of interest and lack of an individualized approach (R88).
- DHH people are between the Deaf and hearing society. I had to decide whether to join the Deaf community and use only sign language or struggle with life through different adaptations (R90).

Attitudes

The attitudes of the teacher and classmates were also identified as a barrier to DHH learners' full participation in English classes. This problem often appeared when the teacher used an inappropriate approach and/or failed to provide sufficient attention; when class members excluded the DHH learner during discussions and group work; and when the teaching involved an unjustified lowering of the requirements for the DHH learner or excessive expectations that he or she would be able to do all the tasks without adaptation to his or her needs:

- I was often overlooked in group discussions (R4).
- I had no support from my teachers in the process of learning (R16).
- In mainstream school, due to my hearing problems, I was not taught pronunciation and I was exempted from oral exams – I wanted to learn to speak correctly, but I didn't know how (R19).

- Why do they always raise their voices instead of accentuating words? I keep telling them that it doesn't help me understand them because it distorts the mouth [such that I cannot lip-read them] (R30).
- I didn't understand people, and they didn't understand me. They had the expectation that because I speak and have hearing aids, I must be able to hear everything and understand (R52).
- People were asked to speak clearly when they talked to me but they quickly forgot. When I asked them to repeat, they tended to say "never mind" or "I'll tell you later". The "later" never came (R67).
- Some teachers and classmates spoke indistinctly, turned their backs on me or had a moustache (R88).
- The teacher didn't know how to help me and didn't take any steps to understand my needs (R86).

Internal barriers

Aside from the external factors, there were also emotional and psychological barriers such as low self-esteem and a lack of self-confidence:

- For a long time I had problems mainly with myself; there was a barrier within me, and it was difficult for me to get out of my comfort zone (R1).
- I was convinced that I shouldn't even bother to speak English if I couldn't use it perfectly and wouldn't reach the level of a hearing person (R3).
- My school thought that I couldn't learn English. So I didn't believe in myself when I used English. After that, it took a long time (with a great effort) to try to speak English (R22).
- I still don't believe I will ever learn it as much as I would like (R23).
- It took me a long time before I tried to speak. I got bullied at school for my English pronunciation. I had difficulty in speaking up for myself, so I had to overcome that first (R29).
- I also have to rely on lip-reading, which is not always a comfortable situation – they notice that I look at their mouths and they react differently to it (R76).

Contact and the use of English

The next most common problem among participants was being unable to become familiar with listening to and speaking English. Sometimes this was caused by the format of their classes and how they were conducted:

- I didn't have the opportunity to properly listen with understanding to the English in class. I was deprived of acquiring an everyday, communicative language (R4).

- I feel a lack of conversational skills when I talk with another person in English because I wasn't included in the discussions in class (R19).
- I cannot listen to the language freely and spontaneously because the teacher didn't make it possible for me to listen to everyday expressions and phrases used in the class (R43).
- I didn't acquire English communication patterns at school, because the teachers spoke and explained mainly in Polish [my native language] instead of English (R74).
- I am less fluent in English because I don't have many opportunities to become familiar with it and be immersed in English (R82).
- There is no practical approach to learning at school – no conversations with native speakers (R85).

This quote sums up in a nutshell the experience of many of the participants:

> In mainstream schools, I was exempted from listening tasks and I didn't have to speak much English. So I didn't have much motivation to learn a foreign language, because for a long time I thought that a person with hearing loss would never be able to speak English fluently or understand by hearing. My thinking changed when I met a girl who attended a school for the deaf . . . , got into English philology studies and graduated [from university]. Now she lives in the UK. Later, I also had the opportunity to meet other DHH people who could communicate in English. Learning English was not easy for them, but it was possible thanks to their determination and the support of others.
>
> (R10)

Positive image of learning a foreign language

It is worth mentioning that the responses often expressed a positive image of learning foreign language too. Many respondents turned their limitations in one area into an advantage in another, thereby not letting their limits hold them back from achieving their goal:

- I realized that because I am hard of hearing I automatically activate the closed captions in every movie if possible, and that this way my reading and writing skills are continually improving alongside hearing/ understanding skills, while many other people are able to communicate well verbally but poorly in a written form (R11).
- I got way less distracted and was therefore able to focus more on the teacher (R55).

- By reading everything, I've learned to write beautifully and have a rich vocabulary (R60).
- Being part of an international hard of hearing organization, which I would otherwise not be part of [if I was not deaf], gives me a higher motivation to learn and work in English (R79).

Discussion

The vast majority of the participants attended mainstream schools. Having DHH individuals in this kind of school and ensuring that they have full access to learning is likely to pose challenges for everyone involved in the teaching and learning process. The school may not have the appropriate facilities and the teacher may not have adequate pedagogical training. The student and their parents may not be aware that learning a foreign language can be realized in such a way that the special needs of DHH learners are met and thus they can be full participants in language classes in accordance with the idea of inclusive education. Also, assumptions of surdo-glottodidactics are related to the contemporary tendencies for the inclusive perception of a place for DHH people in society (Domagała-Zyśk, 2014). DHH people have different experiences of English acquisition, and often their difficulties are not related to their hearing loss, but rather to the maladjustment of the educational environment to their needs. This situation arises when the society is still following a medical model of disability rather than adopting a social one that points out that the environment causes a person's disability (Domagała-Zyśk, 2013).

The assessment of the effectiveness of English classes shows that there is still much room for improvement. English acquisition at a school that follows an organized curriculum needs to be supplemented with additional activities such as extra reading, meeting with others, and travelling abroad. One respondent wrote that *skills require practice* (R90), meaning that a person must also constantly train and expand their knowledge of English through spontaneous daily practice in order to develop their skills. Other respondents wrote *both compliment each other* (R8), and *it's both [that make learning] effective* (R66). Therefore, it should be ensured whenever possible that financial, technical, and human resources are included to enable DHH learners to engage in regular practice and supplemental activities so that they can learn English as effectively as their hearing peers.

Attention should be paid to the possibility of practical and continuous use of English in everyday life, because not only does this support vocabulary, but it also maintains the level of communicative fluency. Even more importantly, it allows the overall level of English to increase much faster – more and more words are learnt, and the sentences become more elaborate and complex. Unfortunately, the number of teaching hours provided to each student may not be enough, and the use of English in class may be limited, which means that the opportunities for practising are insufficient. Often, this approach and the rapid pace at which school peers learn the material means that DHH students are not able to catch up, and as a result the distance between them increases.

There was also an opinion among the participants that learning at school is *typically book-like* (R17) and the curriculum does not fit the reality, because the student may learn many *impractical* (R4) things that are not used on a daily basis. Due to such *dry learning* (R52), the student does not remember much from the classes and is not able to use the knowledge in practice in specific contexts, even though he or she has mastered the vocabulary. One of the respondents noted that the *English used by the teacher is often artificial and too pretentious because most of the time he does not use English* (R87) and the words of another confirm this opinion that the teacher *explained everything in our native language, so we, as students, did not have the chance to learn a natural foreign language and thus break the language barrier that is always present in the absence of contact with English* (R24).

Based on all the statements, it can be concluded that school education should be combined with increased opportunities for using English in practice – then better results can be seen. Such opportunities may be provided by additional activities wherein the learner can be immersed in English and test the skills they acquired at school. Contact with English through reading, watching films, having conversations with foreigners, and travelling abroad helps the learner to shape the specific vocabulary that they need for their own interests and everyday life, and learn to express their own needs *in real-life talk in a genuine environment* (R14). Additional activities in English support DHH learners' motivation to improve their language skills (Domagała-Zyśk & Podlewska, 2019), as well as their successful acquisition. Furthermore, using English in a natural environment is often more interesting than classroom learning, especially if it is to achieve specific goals that are meaningful to the individual learner.

Recommendations for EFL teachers who work with DHH students

To include DHH students in mainstream English classes, it is beneficial to understand what their special needs are and make efforts to ensure that their education is as effective as that of their hearing peers. Therefore, the list that follows offers ten recommendations for teachers who work with DHH students. Only general recommendations can be proposed, because each learner should be approached and observed individually to determine what works in their case and what should be changed. It is worth emphasizing that these recommendations will also benefit the hearing members of the class and increase the quality of EFL teaching for the entire group.

- Talk to the student and their parents about their special needs in terms of learning a foreign language. Do not be afraid to ask questions, because without them it is impossible to take the appropriate steps. Together, identify and evaluate the options that are available.
- Ask the school management for information on the financial resources (e.g. from the government) available to support adaptations for the classroom (e.g. soundproofing, installing an induction loop, or purchasing an FM system).
- Treat each DHH student as an individual, as he or she may have completely different needs than another DHH student. Communication between the individual student and the teacher is important so that the student can be provided with *reasonable accommodation* to his or her needs (e.g. in a listening activity, one student may prefer to look at a written transcript, while another prefers his classmate/teacher to read the transcript to him, and a third student prefers to try to understand the recording herself).
- Adjust the activities so that the DHH student is included. This may involve adapting the teaching techniques, methods, and/or materials (e.g. providing transcripts and ensuring that all videos used in class have subtitles).
- Ensure appropriate environmental accommodation in the classroom, so that DHH students have the best possible access to the subject content and easy contact with other students (e.g. by arranging chairs in a circle to ensure that everyone's face is clearly visible).
- Introduce rules for the class that help DHH students to hear and understand better, such as that everyone must talk one at a time and raise their hand before speaking.
- Use non-formal methods, techniques, technology, and multimedia in the classroom that will provide a variety of activities, increase the amount of visual material (e.g. games, posters, and interactive white boards), and make the lessons more appealing and memorable as content is easier to remember if it is received through multiple stimuli.
- Consult academic literature for guidance and examples of good practice in modifying teaching methods and techniques in foreign language classes to meet the needs of DHH students. This literature will also provide more general knowledge about deafness and DHH people's experiences in education.

- Help DHH students reach out to their deaf peers, for example, through national or international organizations such as the Association of Hard of Hearing People and CI Users SUITA in Poland or the International Federation of Hard of Hearing Young People (IFHOHYP). DHH peers can become role models, show the student that he or she is not alone, and provide support, motivation, and language development opportunities.
- Build links with organizations that provide advice and support for DHH students and advocate for equal access to education and other areas of life. Members of these organizations have useful knowledge and tools to share in the fields of law, technology, education, and social issues.

Notes

1 The word *deaf* written with a lowercase "d" refers to the audiological condition, while *Deaf* with a capital 'D' refers to the people whose first language is a sign language.
2 Although some participants were from English-speaking countries, their first language was not English.
3 According to the BIAP classification, the four degrees of hearing loss are: mild (21–40 dB), moderate (41–70 dB), severe (71–90 dB), and profound (over 91 dB).
4 Data were also gathered on their experiences of using a foreign language abroad, but this part of the research will be presented in a future publication.
5 These questionnaires contained responses about experiences of using English while travelling abroad.

References

Bedoin, D. (2011). English teachers of deaf and hard-of-hearing students in French schools: Needs, barriers and strategies. *European Journal of Special Needs Education, 26*(2), 159–175. https://doi.org/10.1080/08856257.2011.563605

Berent, G. P. (1996). The acquisition of English syntax by deaf learners. In *Handbook of second language acquisition* (pp. 469–506). San Diego: Academic Press.

Connor, C. M., Craig, H. K., Raudenbush, S. W., Heavner, K., & Zwolan, T. A. (2006). The age at which young deaf children receive cochlear implants and their vocabulary and speech-production growth: Is there an added value for early implantation? *Ear and Hearing, 27*(6), 628–644. https://doi.org/10.1097/01. aud.0000240640.59205.42

Csizér, K., & Kontra, E. H. (2020). Foreign language learning characteristics of deaf and severely hard-of-hearing students. *The Modern Language Journal, 104*(1), 233–249. https://doi.org/10.1111/modl.12630

Domagała-Zyśk, E. (2003). Czy istnieje już surdoglottodydaktyka? [Is there already a surdoglottodidactics?]. *Języki Obce w Szkole* [Foreign Languages at School], *4*, 3–7.

Domagała-Zyśk, E. (2012a). Poziom motywacji niesłyszących studentów do uczenia się języków obcych [Motivation of deaf students to learn foreign languages]. In *Student z niepełnosprawnością w środowisku akademickim* [A student with a disability in an academic environment] (pp. 173–200). Cracow: Wyd. św. Stanisława BM.

Domagała-Zyśk, E. (2012b). Strategie nauczania języka angielskiego jako obcego uczniów z uszkodzeniami słuchu w szkołach podstawowych, gimnazjach i szkołach ponadgimnazjalnych [Strategies for teaching English as a foreign language to students with hearing loss in primary, secondary and higher schools]. In *Człowiek – Niepełnosprawność – Społeczeństwo* [Man-Disability-Society] (Vol. 3, pp. 67–85). Warsaw: Wyd. Akademii Pedagogiki Specjalnej im. Marii Grzegorzewskiej.

Domagała-Zyśk, E. (2013). *Wielojęzyczni. Studenci niesłyszący i słabosłyszący w procesie uczenia się i nauczania języków obcych* [Deaf and hard of hearing students in the process of learning and teaching foreign languages]. Lublin: Wyd. KUL.

Domagała-Zyśk, E. (2014). *Surdoglottodydaktyka. Lekcje i zajęcia językowe dla uczniów niesłyszących i słabosłyszących* [Surdoglottodidactics. Language lessons and classes for deaf and hard of hearing students]. Lublin: Wyd. KUL.

Domagała-Zyśk, E. (2015). Kompetencje w zakresie języka angielskiego studentów niesłyszących i słabosłyszących w opinii ich lektorów [English language competences of deaf and hard of hearing students in the opinion of their teachers]. In *Interdyscyplinarne Konteksty Pedagogiki Specjalnej* [Interdisciplinary Contexts of Special Pedagogy] (Vol. 9, pp. 27–44). Poznan: Wyd. Naukowe UAM.

Domagała-Zyśk, E., & Podlewska, A. (2019). Strategies of oral communication of deaf and hard-of-hearing (D/HH) non-native English users. *European Journal of Special Needs Education, 34*(2), 156–171. https://doi.org/10.1080/08856257.20 19.1581399

Krakowiak, K. (2006). Pedagogiczna typologia uszkodzeń słuchu [Pedagogical typology of hearing loss]. In *Krakowiak, K. Przekraczanie barier w wychowywaniu osób z uszkodzeniami słuchu* [Overcoming barriers in educating people with hearing loss] (pp. 255–288). Lublin: Wyd. KUL.

Marschark, M., & Spencer, P. E. (2015). *The Oxford handbook of deaf studies in language*. Oxford: Oxford University Press.

Nowak, S. (2007). *Metodologia badań społecznych* [Methodology of social research] (2nd ed.). Warsaw: Wyd. Naukowe PWN.

Olempska-Wysocka, M. (2016). Rozwój mowy i komunikacji dziecka z uszkodzonym słuchem [Development of the child's with hearing loss speech and communication]. *Interdyscyplinarne Konteksty Pedagogiki Specjalnej* [Interdisciplinary Contexts of Special Pedagogy], *14*, 115–135. https://doi.org/10.14746/ikps.2016.14.07

World Health Organization. (2018). *WHO global estimates on prevalence of hearing loss. Prevention of Deafness WHO, 2018.* Retrieved from shorturl.at/egkn9

Conclusion

Teaching English as a foreign language to DHH learners – future research and practical perspectives

Ewa Domagała-Zyśk, Nuzha Moritz, and Anna Podlewska

The authors hope that this book can be recognized as a significant step forward in developing the methodology of teaching English as a foreign language to deaf and hard of hearing people – as an academic discipline in its own right. With more than 150 scholarly papers so far (cf. www.kul.pl/english-for-deaf-and-hard-of-hearing,art_74431.html), methodology of teaching English as a foreign language to deaf and hard of hearing people (by some of us called surdo-glottodidactic) is becoming a well-established field and providing fertile ground for action research. Nevertheless, each new study brings up even more questions to be answered.

The interventions discussed in this book might have been located within the cluster of comprehensible-input-based methods (Krashen, 1987, 2011). The authors are convinced that DHH students can profit tremendously from acquiring a foreign language, rather than merely learning about it (cf. Krashen, 1987; Domagała-Zyśk, 2013). The key to achieving the benefits of language acquisition are creative strategies that adapt the general methodological rules and principles of EFL to the specific needs of DHH learners. In particular, the book has attempted to shed new light on interventions that can be summarized in the following four recommendations:

1   DHH students learning foreign languages should be offered the possibility to acquire all language skills – listening, reading, writing, and speaking. The scope and intensity of input and practice of each of these skills should be based on recognition of each student's individual needs and biological and social conditions. An English teacher working with DHH students should own a wide repertoire of strategies which might be used in the process of providing comprehensible spoken and written input and helping the student achieve mastery in their writing and speaking output. In Chapter 1, Domagała-Zyśk offered a selection of strategies to support students' speaking skills, like building on habits

from speech therapy, using the Visually Supported Listening protocol, and supporting students' practice of lip-reading, use of speech visualization methods, and uptake of opportunities to converse with supportive native speakers (Krashen, 2011).

2   A high level of phonological awareness is a significant asset for DHH students acquiring both a national (Leybaert, 1993) and a foreign language. However, comprehensible input (Krashen, 1987) for these students needs to be accompanied by visual, tactile, and/or movement cues, as Pritchard suggests in Chapter 2. While recognizing the significance of sign language as a means of communication support, she advocates for establishing phonic reading strategies as early as possible in EFL classes for DHH students.

3   Oral communication for DHH students can be enhanced by carefully selecting practice materials, as learning a foreign language requires meaningful interaction *in the target language* (Krashen, 1994; Mason & Krashen, 2017; Cho, 2017). The strategy of using cartoons, as presented by Moritz in her chapter, follows Krashen's views (cf. Lao & Krashen, 2008) on the kind of material that should be provided for the children. Students' motivation can be developed by choosing the best method that provides "Comprehensible input", like cartoons, comic strips, animated documentaries, or any website prepared with the use of technological tools providing animated images and sounds.

4   Teachers should allow for the fact that nowadays, comprehensible input often involves video materials, whether found on the internet or provided as part of a teaching handbook. While a popular strategy for DHH students might be using traditional reading materials, internet sources seems to fit better with Krashen's comprehensible input and pleasure hypotheses. As Podlewska shows in her chapter, it is possible to adapt video material for DHH students and provide them with both interesting and compelling resources to facilitate their language acquisition.

When teaching strategies are advocated for, questions arise about their effectiveness. The last three chapters of the book reflect on the outputs and outcomes of applying the suggested model of teaching English as a foreign language to deaf and hard of hearing people. Sedláčková stresses the significance of personal variables connected with individual features and motivational issues. Kontra and Lewandowska investigate the students' views. It seems that many DHH young people greatly value EFL programs and see their usefulness in the occupational, cultural, social, and personal spheres. While their communication preferences may vary, with some desiring more signed communication in class (Kontra, Chapter 7) and others wanting more oral communication (Lewandowska's research, Chapter 9),

DHH students' common features are their sense that EFL acquisition will lead to success and that more sophisticated and individualized strategies may enable them to increase their fluency.

The book, though indirectly, poses several new research questions for future reflection. First, since the infancy of surdo-glottodidactics, the authors have been convinced that there should not be a "special" EFL methodology for DHH students. Instead, we need to make use of general, well-developed EFL methodologies, ideally those that exploit the universal learning design model, and provide adjustments and modifications when necessary. More action research is necessary to check the suitability of new language acquisition models for DHH learners.

Secondly, we still know too little about the nature of DHH students' cognitive processes, for example, when they are constructing a word meaning in their mind, comprehending a passage of written text, or memorizing new vocabulary, and how these may be different for signers versus those who prefer oral communication. It is not enough to provide a DHH student with a text and supervise them as they read it; we need to devise ways to investigate how DHH individuals construct meaning when reading texts. To what extent do they use phonological awareness skills? Does usage of these skills depend on their dominant mode of communication which might be oral, signed, or cued? Are there any differences between learners' processes that are based on their national (ethnic/first) language? Research into these issues may bring significant developments to the field of surdo-glottodidactics.

Thirdly, the voice of DHH learners should be heard more vividly. The times have changed dramatically since the late 90s when DHH students were offered foreign language classes for the first time. Nowadays, they are active self-advocates and our collaborators in reforming deaf education. Lewandowska, who is a hard of hearing person herself, uses English as a foreign language with great fluency and works to advance the right of DHH students to access a high-quality education that includes foreign languages. Increasing the number of professionals, practitioners, and academics who are DHH themselves is essential for achieving legitimacy for the field of surdo-glottodidactics and progress in deaf education generally.

References

Cho, J. (2017). English language ideologies in Korea: Interpreting the past and present. Cham: Springer.

Cho, K.-S., & Krashen, S. (1994). Acquisition of Vocabulary from the Sweet Valley Kids Series: Adult ESL Acquisition. Journal of Reading, 37, 662–667.

Domagała-Zyśk, E. (2013). Using technology to teach English as a foreign language to the deaf and hard of hearing. In E. Vilar Beltran, C. Abbott, & J. Jones (Eds.), *Inclusive language education and digital technology* (pp. 84–102). Bristol, London, & Toronto: Multilingual Matters.

Krashen, S. (1987). *Principles and practice in second language acquisition.* Englewood Cliffs, N.J: Prentice-Hall International.

Krashen, S. (2011). The compelling (not just interesting) input hypothesis. *The English Connection (KOTESOL)*, *15*(3), 1.

Lao, C., & Krashen, S. 2008. Heritage language development: Exhortation or good stories? *International Journal of Foreign Language Teaching 4*(2), 17–18.

Leybaert, J. (1993). Reading in the deaf: The role of phonological codes. In M. Marschark & M. D. Clark (Eds.), *Psychological perspective on deafness* (pp. 269–310). Mahwah, NJ: Lawrence Erlbaum Associates.

Mason, B., & Krashen, S. (2017). Self-selected reading and TOEIC performance: Evidence from case histories. *Shitennoji University Bulletin 63*, 469–475.

Index

Note: Page numbers in *italics* indicate a figure and page numbers in **bold** indicate a table on the corresponding page.

access to communication 28
adaptive control of thought (ACT) 3–4
affricatives 20
age 40, 48, 55, 82–83, 86–88
American Sign Language (ASL) 8, 35, 102; *see also* British Sign Language (BSL)
Ammons, D. 95
Anderson, R. C. 3
animated cartoons 48; *see also* cartoons
anxiety 82; and fear 4; level 5
Arnesen, K. 39
articulation 20
articulatory decoding 39
ASL *see* American Sign Language (ASL)
attitudes 21, 120–121
audio-oral methods 2
audio-visual materials 45–46, 119
auditory reception 28
Auge, J. 47
August, D. 33
Avery, T. 49

background noise 55, 76n2
barrier-free education 7
Bedoin, D. 7
behaviorism 1–2
Bossy R 36
Brinkley, D. 55
British Sign Language (BSL) 8, 35; importance of 94–95; in teaching EFL 43n1; *see also* American Sign Language (ASL)

Çakir, I. 50
cartoons 45–46; advantages and drawbacks 48–49; building skills 50–51; classroom implications 49–50; classroom observation experience 49; extrinsic motivation 47–48; intrinsic motivation 45–47; motivation 46; positive impact 47; teaching tools, use as 47–48; use of 47–49
CAWI (computer-assisted web interview) technique 114
Cawthorn, I. 94, 97
centralization of pronunciation of vocal segments 19
chaining method 40
Chambers, G. 94, 97
Children of a Lesser God 71–72
Chomsky, N. 2
Clark, C. 47
clear pronunciation patterns 26
cochlear implants (CIs) 5, 18, 24, 29, 32, 55, 82–83, 110, 113
cognitive performance 82, 88
color code consonants 41
communication: access to 28; e-mail 88; English as tool 22; fluent 110; manual 17; means of 83–84; oral 8, 45, 47–50, 110; second language 3
communicative competence 21
compelling language 4
competence 2; communicative 21; language 4, 21, 29, 85–86, 102

comprehension 33
confidence 5
consonant, short vowel, and consonant (CVC) 36
consonants 20, 36; color code 41; errors 8; pronunciation 20; properties of 39; sounds 20; *see also* vowels
consumerism 55
conversations with native speakers 27
Csuhai, S. 96
cued speech 20–21, 84

D/deaf 96–98, 106, 126n1; community 83; family 87; FL learning 95, 102; FL teachers of 94, 105–106; learners 94, 102; parents 87; sign language in Deaf education 96; teachers of 94; thinking 105–106
deaf and hard of hearing (DHH) people 1, 6; foreign language classes 18, 128; language acquisition 4; national language 2; oral communication 110; quality of speech 19; second language teaching 4–5; sign language 2; speak and understand foreign languages 110; speech pronunciation 19; students learning EFL, difficulties 20, 32; teaching foreign languages 2, 7–10, 18; teaching to speak in foreign language 19
deafness from birth 18
Deci, E. L. 46
declarative knowledge 3
decoding 33
degrees of hearing loss 33, 38, 126n3
DHH people *see* deaf and hard of hearing (DHH) people
digital technology 28
Disney, W. 49
Domagała-Zyśk, E. 8–10, 20, 22, 76n1, 94–95, 112, 128
Donaghy, K. 54
Doring, A. 47
dual-language readers 103
Duolingo application 116

Easterbrooks, S. 76n4
effectiveness in teaching DHH students 45–46; advantages and drawbacks 48–49; building skills 50–51;

cartoons, use of 47–49; classroom implications 49–50; classroom observation experience 49; EFL acquisition 110; extrinsic motivation 47–48; intrinsic motivation 45–47; motivation 46; teaching tools, use as 47–48; use of 47–49
EFL *see* English as foreign language (EFL)
Eilers-crandall, K. 94
elisions 20
Ellis, N. 3
e-mail communication 88
emotionalization 5, 8
English as a foreign language for deaf and hard of hearing persons in Europe 43n1
English: as tool of international communication 22; phonics (L2) 39; speech sounds 32–33, 36; spelling patterns 40
English as foreign language (EFL) 6, 52, 110, 114–115, 128; attitudes 21, 120–121; contact and use of English 121–122; data and methods **113**, 113–114, *115*, **116**; English in everyday life 117; hearing, listening, and understanding, limitations 118–119; internal barriers 121; language, acquisition of 110–111; learner-centered approach 95; learning English 115–117; positive image of learning foreign language 122–123; reasonable accommodation, lack of 120; results 114–123; rules and principles 128; school in DHH learners 111–112; technological and environmental barriers 119–120
English letter names 37
enjoyment 5
equality 10n2
equity 10n2
Estes, E. 76n4
European Federation of Hard of Hearing 114
extrinsic motivation 47–48
extroversion 5

facial expressions 26
Film in Action (Donaghy) 54

films, integration into language courses 54–77; *Children of a Lesser God* 71–72; DHH students 54; EFL 54; *Friends* 68–71; Friendzone Test 66–68; *Frozen* 72–76; *Prom Dress Shopping Fail + Would You Rather!* 63–66; *Signs* 56–60; *Word as Image* 60–62
fingerspelling 27, 39–40, *61*, 62, 84
FL *see* foreign language (FL)
flashcards 42
Fleming, J. 94, 97
fluent communication 110
Fonioková, Z. 8
fonogesty 21
foreign language (FL): education 23; instruction 18; learners 88; learning 6
foreign language teaching: of deaf learners 81; of special needs (SN) learners 93; teaching methodology 10n1
foreign speech 28
foreign spoken language instruction 81
fossilizable linguistic phenomena 3
fossilization 3
fricatives 39
Friends 68–71
Friendzone Test 67–68
Frozen 72–76

genetic engineering 55
gestures 84
Gilmore, A. 47
glottodidactics 10n1
good self-image 5
group motivation 21

habit formation 1
hard of hearing (HOH) 83
hearing aids (HAs) 5, 28
hearing classmates 42
hearing loss: degree of 32; diagnosis 34; learning EFL 34; medical perspective 82–83
Herzig, M. P. 88
hesitations 48
Hughes, P. 56
human intelligence 3
human rights 55
humor 51

Hungarian pronunciation 101
Hungarian Sign Language (HSL) 95, 99

imitation 1, 25, 26, 111
individual differences in second language acquisition 81–82; affective factors 88–89; age factor 86–88; areas of difference 82–85; educational experiences 84–85; hearing loss 82–83; L1 development 85–89; means of communication 83–84
individualization 25, 112
information: gap 41; processing 3–4
intelligibility: of DHH students 22; and language production 20; scores 22
inter-group climate 21
interlanguage 2–3
internal barriers 121
International Federation of Hard of Hearing 114
International Federation of Hard of Hearing Young People 114
International Phonetic Alphabet (IPA) 26, 100
interpersonal motivation 21
intrinsic motivation 45–47
IT-related jobs 103

Karpińska-Szaj, K. 76n1
Katchen, J. E. 48
Keddie, J. 77n7
Kellett Bidoli, C. J. 94
Knoors, H. 85
Kontra, E.H. 6, 94, 129
Krashen, S. 4–6, 129

language: aptitude 82; competences 85; development 34; linguistics, overgeneralization 3; performance 45, 47; skills 128; transfer 2
language acquisition 4, 86; device 2; strategies 5
language learning 4; assessment 37–38; instruments and procedure 36; mainstream learning environment 35; participants 37; pupil 34–35; research aims and objectives 35–36
language teaching methodology for deaf and severely hard-of-hearing

learners 94–95; communicative tasks 99–100; memory strategy, writing as 98–99; reading 102–104; research context 95–96; role of speech and pronunciation 100–101; sign language 104–106; use of written support 97–98
Larsen-Freeman, D. 2
learning: difficulties 93; environment 35; strategies 46, 82
Lee, J. 60
Lewandowska, P. 129
Lightbown, P. 1
linguistic diversity 46
lip movements 39
lip-reading 21, 24–27, 29, 48, 101, 129
lisping 48
Little Red Riding Hood 49

Macurová, A. 85
Madej, E. 77n6
manual communication 17
Marek, B. 17
Marschark, M. 83, 86, 88
MAXQDA 96
McCall, H. 94
media 47
mental block 5
mime 84
mirrors 24
Miskin, R. 40
Mole, J. 94
Montenegro, F. 95
Moritz, N. 8
motivation 5, 45–46, 82; extrinsic 47–48; intrinsic 45–47; to learn and to speak 22
movement 38
multilingualism 110
multimedia 28
multi-sensory information 32

nasal sounds 39
native speakers, conversations with 27
natural language development 85
Network of Expert Centers Providing Inclusion in Tertiary Education 22
neutral vowel schwa 20
non-stop paper switch 41

Norwegian: phonic reading (L1) 39; speech sounds 37
Norwegian National Curriculum in English for Pupils with Sign Language 34, 36

Ochse, E. 94
online chat 88
oral communication 8, 45, 47–50

Padden, C. 102
Paivio, A. 76n6
paralinguistic features 48
Parasnis, I. 46
Parrott, T. 51
performance 2
personality traits 21
personalization strategy 4
phonemes 33
phonetic transcription 100
phonic information 39
phonic reading to EFL 32–33; challenges 34–36; as foreign language and DHH pupils 33–34; instruments and procedure 36; participants 37; results of assessment 37–38; teaching strategies 38–42
phonic text, reading aloud 37
phonological awareness (PA) 32–33
Piñar, P. 95
pleasure hypothesis 5
plosives 39
Podlewska, A. 9–10, 21–22, 26, 76n1
positive reinforcement 112
prelingual deafness 83
Pritchard, P. 8, 95
procedural knowledge 3
proficiency in foreign languages 117, *117*
Prom Dress Shopping Fail + Would You Rather! 63–66
pronunciation 25–26; accuracy 19; *ed* suffix 23; English 25; foreign language 26; instruction 23; intelligibility 22; performance 19; voiced and voiceless /th/ 23; *see also* speech and pronunciation
pupil: exposure 35; motivation 34

racism 55
Rae, L. 47
Ramsey, C. 102
Read Aloud assessment test 36
reading: English as foreign language
    33–34; and writing 84
Red-Hot Riding Hood 49
reverberation 55, 76n3
Roos, C. 39
Rule, A. C. 47
Ryan, R. M. 46

sealant 55
second language acquisition (SLA) 1,
    86; behaviorism 1–2; information
    processing 3–4; interlanguage
    2–3; language acquisition device
    2; Stephen Krashen's theory 4–6;
    strategies of 3
second language communication 3
Sedláčková, J. 8, 95, 102, 129
self-confidence 21
self-correction 5
Selinker, L. 2–3
sensory accessibility of sign language 86
sensory impairments 93
Shanahan, T. 33
sibilants 20
sight-reading 37
sign language 27, 83–84, 87; in Deaf
    education 96; importance of 94;
    sensory accessibility of 86; use of 104
Signs 56–60
Skinner, B.F. 1, 2
SLA *see* second language acquisition
    (SLA)
sonority 20
sound-symbol correspondence 100
Spada, N. 1
speaking in foreign language 18, 28
special educational needs (SEN) 55,
    81, 93
speech 84; intelligibility 8, 19;
    production rules 23; reading 24–25;
    recognition 21; sounds 38; therapy
    classes 23–24; visualization 26–27
speech and pronunciation 17–18;
    conversations with native
    speakers 27; digital technology 28;
    English pronunciation 18–21;

lip-reading 24–25; motivation and
    willingness 21–22; pronunciation
    25–26; speaking 28; speech
    therapy habits 23–24; speech
    visualization methods 26–27;
    visually supported listening 24; at
    work 23–29
speech-to-text transliteration 26
speed sound poster 40
spelling patterns 32–33, 40
Spencer, P.E. 86
spoken language: development 18;
    differences with signs language 83–85
stammering 48
Subtitle Edit 55
supra-segmental articulatory errors 8
surdo-glottodidactics 1, 6–7, 111, 130
Sutherland, I. M. 76n5
systematic teaching 33

tactile and visual clues 39
teaching: British Sign Language (BSL)
    in 8, 35, 43n1, 94–95; cartoons
    47–48; foreign languages 2, 7–10,
    18; oral communication 45; second
    language 4–5; specialism 18;
    strategies 38–42; systematic 33;
    see also effectiveness in teaching
    DHH students; foreign language
    teaching; language teaching
    methodology for deaf and severely
    hard-of-hearing learners
traditional error correction 5
transfer of training 2

unnatural-sounding voices 48
unsystematic acquisition 87

Vale, M. 94
video captioning 55
visible and invisible articulations 39
visual articulation 48
visual contact 112
visual-gestural character 83
visualization of speech sounds 26
visually supported listening 24, 129
visual modality 46
Visual Phonics 20–21, 84
visual sense 38
vlog 63–66

vocabulary: learning 60; personalization 8
voiced and unvoiced sounds 39
voice frequency 48
vowels: pronunciation 19–20; spelling patterns 36; *see also* consonants

Web Content Accessibility Guidelines (WCAG) 28
willingness to communicate 21–22; in English as foreign language 22; scale 22

Word as Image 60–62
word forming English speech sounds 41
word pictures, memorizing 37
words, semantic and morphological analysis of 8
World Health Organization 82–83
written language 33

YOLO (*you only live once*) 65

Zabrocki, L. 10n1